Workbook to Accompany

# Today's Health Information Management: An Integrated Approach

## Workbook to Accompany
# Today's Health Information Management: An Integrated Approach

by
**Dana C. McWay, JD, RHIA**

Prepared by
**Joanne Valerius**

DELMAR
CENGAGE Learning

Australia • Brazil • Japan • Korea • Mexico • Singapore • Spain • United Kingdom • United States

**Workbook to Accompany Today's Health Information Management: An Integrated Approach**
Dana C. McWay

Vice President, Health Care Business Unit:
William Brottmiller

Director of Learning Solutions: Matthew Kane

Senior Acquisitions Editor: Rhonda Dearborn

Product Manager: Sarah Prime

Editorial Assistant: Laura Pye

Marketing Director: Jennifer McAvey

Marketing Coordinator: Andrea Eobstel

Technology Director: Laurie Davis

Technology Product Manager:
Mary Colleen Liburdi

Technology Project Manager: Carolyn Fox

Production Director: Carolyn Miller

Content Project Manager: Jessica McNavich

Art Director: Jack Pendleton

For product information and technology assistance, contact us at
**Cengage Learning Customer & Sales Support, 1-800-354-9706**
For permission to use material from this text or product,
submit all requests online at **www.cengage.com/permissions**
Further permissions questions can be emailed to
**permissionrequest@cengage.com**

ISBN-13: 978-1-4180-0146-9

ISBN-10: 1-4180-0146-5

**Delmar**
Executive Woods
5 Maxwell Drive
Clifton Park, NY 12065
USA

Cengage Learning is a leading provider of customized learning solutions with office locations around the globe, including Singapore, the United Kingdom, Australia, Mexico, Brazil, and Japan. Locate your local office at **www.cengage.com/global**

Cengage Learning products are represented in Canada by Nelson Education, Ltd.

To learn more about Delmar, visit **www.cengage.com/delmar**

Purchase any of our products at your local bookstore or at our preferred online store **www.cengagebrain.com**

**Notice to the Reader**
Publisher does not warrant or guarantee any of the products described herein or perform any independent analysis in connection with any of the product information contained herein. Publisher does not assume, and expressly disclaims, any obligation to obtain and include information other than that provided to it by the manufacturer. The reader is expressly warned to consider and adopt all safety precautions that might be indicated by the activities described herein and to avoid all potential hazards. By following the instructions contained herein, the reader willingly assumes all risks in connection with such instructions. The publisher makes no representations or warranties of any kind, including but not limited to, the warranties of fitness for particular purpose or merchantability, nor are any such representations implied with respect to the material set forth herein, and the publisher takes no responsibility with respect to such material. The publisher shall not be liable for any special, consequential, or exemplary damages resulting, in whole or part, from the readers' use of, or reliance upon, this material.

Printed in the United States of America
3 4 5 6 7 14 13 12 11

# CONTENTS

# TO THE LEARNER

The Workbook helps you learn and reinforce the essential concepts presented in the book. You will be asked to recall abbreviations, vocabulary, and key concepts presented in the text as part of each assignment sheet. Test your knowledge of each chapter through multiple choice and true/false quizzes, short answer questions, and similar activities.

## Critical Thinking

Critical thinking skills are vital to success in the health information management field. Employ critical thinking for the "Case Exploration" scenarios in the assignment sheets. Often a specific scenario will be presented, and you will be asked how you would respond.

## The StudyWARE Challenge

StudyWARE is interactive software on the student CD-ROM found in the back of the textbook. The software includes learning activities and quizzes to help study key concepts and test your comprehension. The activity and quiz content corresponds with each chapter of the book. Throughout this Workbook you will be asked to complete specific activities or quizzes using your StudyWARE software, which will provide you with a multimedia learning experience.

## The DVD Hookup

The "DVD Hookup" feature suggests scenes from the *Case Studies for Health Information Management* DVD series available from Delmar, Cengage Learning. This series focuses on applying critical thinking skills to real events and situations that occur in the workplace. Each case study dramatizes a real situation, provides a discussion checkpoint, and follows with an outcome that reflects how the scenario would be resolved in the real world. On each assignment sheet in this Workbook, you will be asked to respond to questions related to these scenarios.

# Assignment Sheets

# CHAPTER 1

# Health Care Delivery Systems

## Learning Objectives

1. Trace the historical development of the health care delivery system in early times.

2. Describe the four-stage progression of the health care delivery system in the United States.

3. Describe the increase in stature of hospitals after World War II.

4. Explain the standardization movement of the early 20th century.

5. Define the term *accreditation* and explain its significance to health care organizations.

6. Compare and contrast the federal government's role in health care during stages three and four.

7. Define the concept of managed care and differentiate between the three main types.

8. Trace the historical development of public, mental, and occupational health.

9. Compare and contrast professional associations, voluntary health agencies, philanthropic foundations, and international health agencies.

10. Differentiate between the variety of settings where health care is delivered.

11. Compare and contrast physicians, dentists, chiropractors, podiatrists, optometrists, physician assistants, nurses, and allied health professionals.

12. Understand the organization of a hospital's medical staff, the importance of its bylaws, and the use of the credentialing process in granting clinical privileges.

## Acronym Review

Write out the following acronyms.

1. PHI: _____

2. HIPAA: _____

3. ONCHIT: _____

4. EHR: _____

5. AHIMA: _____

6. AMA: _____

7. AHA: _____

8. BCBS: _____

9. DRG: _____

10. DHHS: _____

# Key Terms Review

Match the terms in Column I to their definitions in Column II.

| | Column I | | Column II |
|---|---|---|---|
| 1. _____ | Accreditation | A. | The permission granted and the limits set by a hospital's governing board that allow the physician to treat patients at the hospital. |
| 2. _____ | Board certified | B. | A form of managed care; a community-based group of independent practitioners who contract to provide care for prepaid, enrolled individuals. |
| 3. _____ | Capitation | C. | The action of a nongovernmental entity (e.g., a professional association) to recognize those individuals who meet specified standards (e.g., education and experience). |
| 4. _____ | Clinical privileges | D. | A specialty board of physicians has determined through rigorous examination that the specialist may limit her practice due to her advanced training and demonstration of competence. |
| 5. _____ | Continuum of care | E. | Nongovernmental organizations created to perform public work in health care through private means. |
| 6. _____ | HMO | F. | The care provided by the health care professional at the initial point of contact and in the coordination of all aspects of the patient's health care. |
| 7. _____ | IPA | G. | A form of managed care; a network of participating hospitals, physicians, medical groups, and other providers who contract with a sponsor to provide services to those enrolled. |
| 8. _____ | Managed care | H. | A program designed to provide financing for health care for all persons over age 65, regardless of financial need. |
| 9. _____ | Medicaid | I. | Health plans that integrate fully the financial and delivery aspects of health care. |
| 10. _____ | Medicare | J. | The process by which an external entity reviews an organization or program of study to determine if the organization or program meets certain predetermined standards. |
| 11. _____ | Outsourcing | K. | A form of managed care; a prepaid, organized system for providing comprehensive health care services within a geographic area to all persons under contract, emphasizing preventive medicine. |
| 12. _____ | PPO | L. | The concept of matching individuals with the appropriate level and type of health, social, psychological, or medical care of service within an organization or across multiple organizations. |
| 13. _____ | Primary care | M. | The delegation of non-care operations from internal production of a business to an external entity that specializes in an operation. |
| 14. _____ | Registration | N. | A program designed to provide financing for health care of poor or impoverished persons. |
| 15. _____ | Voluntary health agencies | O. | A payment method using a fixed amount per member per month to a contracted provider for health care services, regardless of the quantity or nature of the services rendered. |

## True or False

Indicate whether the following statements are true (T) or false (F). If a statement is false, rewrite it to make it true.

1. _____ At the federal level, the cause of occupational health is overseen by the Occupational Safety and Health Administration (OSHA).

   _____

2. _____ Managed care means the patient takes care of his or her own health care.

   _____

3. _____ Accreditation is the process in which an external group determines whether an organization meets predetermined standards.

   _____

4. _____ IPA is the abbreviation for independent practice association.

   _____

5. _____ PPO refers to professional podiatrist organizations.

   _____

6. _____ There is written proof of physicians and dentists as early as 2700 B.C.

   _____

7. _____ Licensing refers to a right conferred by the government to practice.

   _____

8. _____ Medicare is designed to provide financing for health care of poor or impoverished persons.

   _____

9. _____ Three types of managed care include HMO, IPA, and PPO.

   _____

10. _____ Outsourcing non-encrypted data violates HIPAA.

    _____

11. _____ In 1982, Congress passed the Tax Equity and Fiscal Responsibility Act (TEFRA).

    _____

## Multiple Choice

Select the best response.

1. The consumer culture emerged because of:

   A) Increased levels of education in the United States

   B) Increased demands for higher quality of care

C) Increased demands for preventative care

D) All of the above

2. The development of public health includes:

A) Improving community health

B) Preventative care in sanitation

C) Curing chronic disease

D) All of the above

3. The credential process for physicians:

A) Is based only on hospital standards

B) Grants clinical privileges per a governing body

C) Relies on the physician to disclose malpractice claims

D) Is decided by the medical credentialing specialist

4. Managed care:

A) Is prepaid

B) Emphasizes preventive medicine

C) Uses capitation to pay physicians

D) All of the above

5. HMOs:

A) Use a preestablished discount for payment

B) Utilize a contracted fee basis

C) Use a capitation method

D) Use a fee-for-services payment system

6. TEFRA:

A) Introduced the concept of the prospective payment system (PPS)

B) Limited reimbursement using diagnosis-related groups (DRGs)

C) Introduced managed care

D) Both A and B

## Short Answer

1. Outline the historical development of public health as described in this chapter.

17th century: _____

17th–20th century: _____

_____

_____

20th century–1945: _____

_____

_____

_____

1945–2000: _____

_____

_____

_____

_____

_____

2. Describe the services provided at the federal, state, and local levels in terms of public health as described in this chapter.

Federal level: _____

_____

_____

_____

_____

State level: _____

_____

Local level: _____

_____

3. Describe the two categories of health information professionals.

_____

_____

4. How does a nursing home differ from a skilled nursing facility?

_____

_____

_____

_____

_____

5. What is the difference between a rehabilitation hospital and a rehabilitation care facility?

_____

_____

_____

6. Is accreditation mandatory?

_____

_____

_____

7. Is a professional (e.g., a nurse) who is licensed in one state permitted to work in a neighboring state?

_____

_____

_____

_____

_____

## The StudyWARE™ Challenge

Using the StudyWARE on your student software CD-ROM, complete the following activities:

1. Study the flash cards for Chapter 1 to review the key terms in this chapter.

2. Solve the crossword puzzle for Chapter 1.

3. Complete the quiz in test mode for Chapter 1. Record your score in the space below, and print out your results for your instructor.

| |
|---|
| **StudyWARE Quiz Chapter 1** |
| Date Taken: _____ |
| Score: _____ |

## The DVD Hookup

Program 3: Health Services Organization and Delivery

Case 3.2: Delinquent Medical Records and JCAHO

The HIM director and quality improvement coordinator are meeting to discuss preparation for a Joint Commission visit in respect to HIM department compliance reporting. The objective of this scenario is to think about the complexity of the calculations required by Joint Commission accreditation.

## Case Discussion

1. What should be included as part of the operative rate?

_____

_____

2. What can be done to reduce the number of delinquent medical records?

_____

_____

_____

_____

_____

3. Do Keeler and King's reactions surprise you? Why or why not?

_____

_____

_____

4. Since what they are doing is not working, what else could they do to help reach a decision about what to include in the denominator?

_____

# CHAPTER 2

# The Health Information Management Profession

## Learning Objectives

1. Define the terms *health record* and *health information.*

2. Trace the development of the American Health Information Management Association and its predecessor organizations.

3. List and describe activities of the American Health Information Management Association in the 20th century.

4. Understand the organizational structure of the American Health Information Management Association.

5. Explain the educational and certification requirements of the health information management profession.

6. Identify the change in career roles of the health information management professional from the last half of the 20th century to present day.

7. List and describe the various roles played by the health information management professional in a traditional setting.

8. Explain the role of the health information management professional in selected nontraditional settings.

## Acronym Review

Write out the following acronyms.

1. CHP: _____

2. CHS: _____

3. CHPS: _____

4. CCS: _____

5. CCS-P: _____

6. CCA: _____

7. RHIT: _____

8. RHIA: _____

9. FAHIMA: _____

## Key Terms Review

Match the terms in Column I to their definitions in Column II.

| | **Column I** | | **Column II** |
|---|---|---|---|
| 1. _____ | Health care informatics | A. | An ordered set of documents, in the paper context, or a collection of data, in an electronic context, that contains a complete and accurate description of a patient's history, condition, diagnostic and therapeutic treatment, and results of treatment. |
| 2. _____ | Quality assurance | B. | The meaningful data relating to the health of an individual that is created or received by a health care provider, health plan, public health authority, employer, life insurer, school or university, or health care clearinghouse. |
| 3. _____ | Health record | C. | The unique contribution of an activity is measured by the difference between the original component materials and the finished work product. |
| 4. _____ | Health information | D. | Provides leadership, networking, and professional education opportunities for AHIMA members. |
| 5. _____ | Managed care | E. | Those actions taken to establish, protect, promote, and improve the quality of health care. |
| 6. _____ | Communities of practice | F. | Involves the process of comparing preestablished criteria against the health care provided to the patient to determine whether that care is necessary. |
| 7. _____ | Utilization review | G. | A discipline focused on studying both the structure and general properties of information and the designing and implementation of technology to use and communicate that information. |
| 8. _____ | Value-added concept | H. | The delegation of non-care operations from internal production of a business to an external entity that specializes in an operation. |
| 9. _____ | Component state associations | I. | A Web-based program that provides a virtual network for AHIMA members who share common interests. |
| 10. _____ | Outsourcing | J. | Health plans that integrate fully the financial and delivery aspects of health care. |

## True or False

Indicate whether the following statements are true (T) or false (F). If a statement is false, rewrite it to make it true.

1. _____ Communities of Practice (CoP) are networks of professionals who learn from one another.

_____

2. _____ Component state associations (CSAs) are health information associations found in each state.

_____

3. _____ The executive director of AHIMA manages day-to-day operations.

_____

4. _____ The board of directors of AHIMA advises the House of Delegates.

_____

## Matching

Match the job titles in Column I to their descriptions in Column II.

**Column I**

1. _____ Data analysts

2. _____ Document and repository manager

3. _____ Medical transcription

4. _____ Privacy Officer

5. _____ Security Officer

6. _____ Tumor registrar

7. _____ Utilization review coordinators

8. _____ Quality assurance coordinators

9. _____ Admissions coordinators

10. _____ Medical staff coordinators

11. _____ Risk managers

12. _____ Clinical research associates

**Column II**

A. Develops and implements policies and procedures related to the HIPAA Security Rule; accountable for a covered entity's security procedures.

B. Assist in the design, implementation, and monitoring of clinical research studies, including the design of data collection instructions and preparation of reports concerning study findings.

C. Coordinate the activities of a health care provider's office, including the health information, personnel, finance, insurance, and risk management functions.

D. Measure and assess the quality of clinical and patient-care services and offer recommendations for improvement.

E. Act of transcribing prerecorded dictation to create medical reports, correspondence, and other administrative material.

F. Review health care claims for medical necessity and reasonableness of costs.

G. Coordinate the coding and claims processing functions associated with revenue cycle management.

H. Direct the patient registration functions, setting guidelines for preregistration and registration of patients and managing the computerized registration process.

I. Develops and implements policies and procedures related to the HIPAA Privacy Rule and serves as the covered entity's point of contact to receive complaints; disseminates information about the entity's privacy practices.

J. Responsible for ensuring long-term data integrity and access through the development of retention policies and procedures, determination of appropriate media for data and record storage, and maintenances of data control inventories.

K. Direct the credentialing process of physicians and allied health staff of an organization.

L. Act to reduce medical, financial, and legal risk to an organization through investigation, analysis, and recommendations for corrective action.

| 13. _____ | Health insurance specialists | M. | Identifies, collects, and maintains information about tumors, including cancer, that are diagnosed and/or treated by an organization. |
|---|---|---|---|
| 14. _____ | Charge description master coordinators | N. | Coordinate the delivery of health care, whether on a departmental or an organization-wide basis. |
| 15. _____ | Health service managers | O. | Responsible for analyzing records and data quantitatively and qualitatively. |
| 16. _____ | Medical office managers | P. | Compare preestablished criteria against the health care provided to the patients to determine whether that care was necessary, and communicate those results using narrative and graphical reports. |

## Short Answer

1. What does the term *health record* mean? What are some other names for the health record?

_____

_____

_____

_____

2. What does the term *health information* mean? What are some examples of health information?

_____

_____

_____

3. Trace the development of AHIMA, listing activities of the organization.

1928: _____

_____

1938: _____

_____

1970: _____

_____

1991: _____

_____

_____

4. Identify career roles of HIM professionals from 1950 to 1999.

_____

_____

5. Identify career roles of HIM professionals from 2000 to the present.

_____

_____

6. List the traditional setting(s) in which HIM professionals are employed.

_____

7. List several nontraditional roles or settings for HIM professionals.

_____

_____

8. What is the difference between medical library science and HIM?

_____

_____

_____

_____

9. What is the difference between health care informatics and HIM?

_____

_____

_____

10. What are the three purposes derived from the AHIMA e-HIM work?

(1) _____

(2) _____

(3) _____

11. Review the employment settings in Table 2–5 and the discussion about roles of HIM professionals. Choose two of the settings listed and describe what the role of an HIM in each setting would include.

_____

_____

_____

_____

_____

_____

_____

_____

## The StudyWARE™ Challenge

Using the StudyWARE on your student software CD-ROM, complete the following activities:

1. Study the flash cards for Chapter 2 to review the key terms in this chapter.

2. Complete the hangman activities for Chapter 2.

3. Complete the quiz in test mode for Chapter 2. Record your score in the space below, and print out your results for your instructor.

> **StudyWARE Quiz Chapter 2**
>
> Date Taken: _____
>
> Score: _____

# CHAPTER 3

# Legal Issues

## Learning Objectives

1. Differentiate between law, regulations, rules, requirements, and standards.

2. Compare and contrast the roles of governmental entities in health care.

3. Explain the roles of nongovernmental entities in health care.

4. Compare and contrast the court system with administrative bodies.

5. List and describe the principles of liability.

6. Understand the goals of administrative simplification and combating fraud and abuse under the Health Insurance Portability and Accountability Act.

7. Explain the interrelationship between confidentiality and privacy.

8. Discuss the principles of ownership and disclosure of health information.

9. Define the informed consent doctrine and discuss its relationship to advance directives.

10. Compare and contrast a court order authorizing disclosure of health information with a subpoena.

11. Understand the concept of fraud and abuse, the underlying statutory mechanisms supporting the concept, and the resources available to combat it.

## Acronym Review

Write out the following acronyms.

1. CMS: _____

2. CDC: _____

3. SSA: _____

4. AHRQ: _____

5. NIH: _____

6. OSHA: _____

7. NLRB: _____

8. DOJ: _____

## Key Terms Review

Match the terms in Column I to their definitions in Column II.

| | **Column I** | | **Column II** |
|---|---|---|---|
| 1. _____ | Law | A. | Those things considered necessary, obligatory, or demanded as a condition. |
| 2. _____ | Regulations | B. | Refers to conduct the government has declared injurious to the public order, with specific punishments identified for violations. |
| 3. _____ | Rules | C. | Decisions and regulations issued by government agencies that are charged with interpreting statutory law. |
| 4. _____ | Requirements | D. | Laws that arise from the actions of municipal bodies. |
| 5. _____ | Standards | E. | Refers to conflicts between private parties. |
| 6. _____ | Private law | F. | Prescribed courses of action that arise from law, principle, or custom. |
| 7. _____ | Public law | G. | Provisions found in the U.S. Constitution that are considered superior or supreme above laws from other sources. |
| 8. _____ | Criminal law | H. | Body of rules of action or conduct prescribed by a controlling authority that has binding legal force. |
| 9. _____ | Civil law | I. | Laws created by the legislative branches of federal and state governments. |
| 10. _____ | Constitutional law | J. | Criteria established as a basis for comparing matters such as quantity, quality, value, or weight. |
| 11. _____ | Statutory law | K. | Generally defined as that part of the law that does not include criminal law. |
| 12. _____ | Ordinances | L. | Refers to conflicts between the government and private parties or between two or more branches of government. |
| 13. _____ | Administrative law | M. | Principles established by authorities, prescribing or directing certain action or forbearance from action. |
| 14. _____ | Executive orders | N. | Refers to the division of power between the branches of government. |
| 15. _____ | Common law | O. | Issued by the chief executive at either the federal or state level; used to interpret or implement a provision of a constitution or law. |
| 16. _____ | Separation of powers | P. | Judicial decisions that interpret relevant constitutional provisions, federal or state statutes, regulations, and/or previous court decisions. |

## True or False

Indicate whether the following statements are true (T) or false (F). If a statement is false, rewrite it to make it true.

1. _____ *Jurisdiction* refers to the authority of a court to hear a case.

_____

2. _____ Trial courts may have different names depending on whether they are deciding a federal or state case.

_____

3. _____ The U.S. Supreme Court only hears appeals brought from the federal appellate courts.

_____

4. _____ Administrative bodies are part of the judicial system.

_____

5. _____ OSHA and NLRB both deal with workplace issues.

_____

6. _____ CDC is the same as the U.S. Department of Health and Human Services.

_____

7. _____ In every lawsuit, there is a plaintiff and a defendant.

_____

8. _____ Defendants bring a lawsuit against a plaintiff.

_____

9. _____ Plaintiffs are responsible for initiating a lawsuit.

_____

10. _____ The *complaint* is filed by the plaintiff.

_____

## Multiple Choice

Select the best response.

1. HIPAA is administered by:

    A) CMS

    B) SSA

    C) Civil rights agencies

    D) CDC

2. The CMS:

    A) Administers Medicare and Medicaid services

    B) Is located within the U.S. Department of Health and Human Services

    C) Is responsible for administering HIPAA

    D) All of the above

3. The NIH:

    A) Does biomedical research

    B) Develops rules concerning protection in human research

    C) Is an agency of the federal government

    D) All of the above

4. The DOJ:

    A) Prosecutes civil and criminal law

    B) Oversees mergers of health care entities

    C) Prosecutes fraud and abuse

    D) All of the above

5. The CDC:

    A) Receives mandatory reporting from health care agencies

    B) Prosecutes fraud and abuse

    C) Develops rules about human research

    D) Is responsible for HIPAA violations

6. In a lawsuit, the complaint describes:

    A) The jurisdiction of the court

    B) Grounds for the lawsuit

    C) The type of relief the plaintiff wants

    D) All of the above

7. Discovery is the time that:

    A) Pretrial preparation occurs

    B) Comes before the complaint

    C) Does not include e-discovery

    D) Does not include metadata

## Matching

Choose the correct acronym from the list below for each sentence that follows.

A.  AHRQ

B.  CDC

C.  CMS

D.  DOJ

E.  NIH

F.  OSHA

G.  NLRB

H.  SSA

1.  _____ Prosecutes civil and criminal law violations.

2.  _____ Prevents and remedies unfair labor practices at work.

3.  _____ Administers Medicare and Medicaid.

4.  _____ Administers programs for the prevention of communicable diseases.

5.  _____ Federal government's principle biomedical research agency.

6.  _____ Provides research about health care outcomes, quality, cost, and access.

7.  _____ Focuses on safe working conditions.

8.  _____ Administers the Social Security program.

## Multiple Response

Place an X next to all of the correct answers.

In the discovery phase of a lawsuit, the following need to be available to both parties of the lawsuit when requested:

_____ A.  Depositions

_____ B.  Written interrogatories

_____ C.  Production of documents

_____ D.  Physical evidence

_____ E.  Subpoenas

_____ F.  Physical examinations

_____ G.  Mental examinations

_____ H. Business records

_____ I. Medical records

_____ J. Electronic documents

## Short Answer

1. What are the intentional torts mentioned in the text? Provide an example of each.

_____

_____

_____

2. List four uses of the medical record for legal purposes.

_____

_____

_____

3. Explain the interrelationship between confidentiality and privacy.

_____

_____

_____

4. What does *informed consent* mean?

_____

_____

## The StudyWARE™ Challenge

Using the StudyWARE on your student software CD-ROM, complete the following activities:

1. Study the flash cards for Chapter 3 to review the key terms in this chapter.
2. Solve the hangman activities for Chapter 3.
3. Complete the quiz in test mode for Chapter 3. Record your score in the space below, and print out your results for your instructor.

> **StudyWARE Quiz Chapter 3**
>
> Date Taken: _____
>
> Score: _____

## The DVD Hookup

Program 1: Health Data Management

Case 1.2: Fulfilling a Subpoena for the Record of a Deceased Patient

The ROI receptionist pays a visit to the HIM director to ask about fulfilling a subpoena for a certified copy of a death record. This scenario involves compliance with state laws concerning release of information and the practical aspects of (1) how to handle a subpoena; and (2) how to handle a request for production of document. Compliance with this scenario requires knowledge of the American College of Surgeons (ACS) standards on documentation requirements for completed autopsy reports to patient records, the Joint Commission standards on autopsy documentation, and the hospital's compliance plan concerning HIPAA with regard to privacy and security of patient records.

## Case Discussion

1. What are the documentation standards for completion of records?

 

2. What are the legal ramifications of an incomplete record?

 

3. Why would you want Risk Management to review the record?

Program 2: Health Statistics, Biomedical Research, and Quality Management

Case 2.4: The Hallway Incident

A coder comes to the aid of a hospital visitor who is unconscious on the floor. When you work in a health care facility, you never know what to expect; a lot of people go in and out of the facility. An HIM professional could find himself or herself the first person on the scene when a patient falls or has a myocardial infarction.

## Case Discussion

1. If you were a hospital employee, how would you have responded?

_____

_____

2. How should the incident be investigated? What are some questions that might be asked of the victim?

_____

_____

_____

_____

3. If the staff failed to respond to the visitor's fall, how could their jobs be impacted? How could the hospital be impacted?

_____

_____

_____

_____

4. Why was the health information staff member (coder) responsible for assisting the visitor who had fallen?

_____

_____

_____

Program 3: Health Services Organization and Delivery

Case 3.3: Assessing the Compliance Plan

The HIM director, business office director, and compliance officer meet for a reality check about the effectiveness of their compliance plan. Periodically reviewing the plan is critical to make sure that it complies with current standards. Typically, facilities will have a compliance officer in charge of ensuring that the facility complies with regulations and its own policies and procedures.

## Case Discussion

1. Identify the problems that are presented in this case. What action should the committee take?

_____

_____

_____

_____

_____

2. How can they get people to follow the plan? How often should it be evaluated?

_____

_____

_____

_____

3. Why is compliance so important?

_____

_____

_____

_____

# CHAPTER 4

# Ethical Standards

## Learning Objectives

1. Differentiate between ethics, morals, values, etiquette, and law.

2. Compare and contrast ethical concepts and theories.

3. Understand the ethical decision-making process.

4. Define codes of ethics and discuss their importance.

5. Restate the dilemmas posed by bioethical issues.

6. Identify ethical challenges in general and their application to the role of supervision, the field of health care, and the specialized area of health information management.

## Acronym Review

Write out the following acronyms.

1. PSDA: _____

2. HIPAA: _____

3. HIV: _____

4. AIDS: _____

5. HGP: _____

6. DNR: _____

## Key Terms Review

Match the terms in Column I to their definitions in Column II.

| | Column I | | Column II |
|---|---|---|---|
| 1. _____ | Autonomy | A. | An ethical concept referring to the prohibition against doing harm; operates through the obligation to prevent evil or harm. |
| 2. _____ | Beneficence | B. | An ethical concept referring to faithfulness, loyalty, and devotion to one's obligations or duties. |
| 3. _____ | Nonmaleficence | C. | An ethical concept referring to independence, self-determination, or freedom. |

4. _____     Double effect principle

     D.   An ethical concept referring to the obligation to be fair to all people.

5. _____     Best interests standard

     E.   An ethical concept referring to the qualities of kindness, mercy, and charity.

6. _____     Fidelity

     F.   An ethical concept referring to the fair distribution of burdens and benefits using an independent standard.

7. _____     Justice

     G.   An ethical concept used when determining what is in the best interest of an individual when the individual cannot make such a decision herself.

8. _____     Comparative justice

     H.   An ethical concept referring to balancing the competing interests of individuals and groups against each other, with no independent standard used to make the comparison.

9. _____     Distributive justice

     I.   A just claim or entitlement, whether based on law, ethics, or morality, that others are obliged to respect.

10. _____     Rights

     J.   A principle that recognizes that ethical choices may result in untoward outcomes.

## True or False

Indicate whether the following statements are true (T) or false (F). If a statement is false, rewrite it to make it true.

1. _____ Values are the formal study of moral choices that conform to standards of conduct.

_____

2. _____ Ethics are recognized as the principles or fundamental standards of "right" conduct.

_____

3. _____ Ethical acts are like laws, in which actions or conduct have the binding force of legality.

_____

4. _____ Laws are created as a means to control behavior and protect the public from danger.

_____

5. _____ Values are the concepts that give meaning to an individual's life and serve as the framework for decision making.

_____

6. _____ Ethics are the concepts that give meaning to an individual's life and serve as the framework for decision making.

_____

7. _____ Privacy and confidentiality have a legal and ethical base.

_____

8. _____ Confidentiality is the obligation of the health care provider to maintain patient information in a manner that will not permit dissemination beyond the health care provider.

9. _____ Privacy refers to the right to be left alone or the right to control personal information.

10. _____ Ethical behavior refers to habitual truthfulness and honesty.

11. _____ Veracity refers to habitual truthfulness and honesty.

12. _____ Withholding treatment at the end of life is based upon the concepts of autonomy and the right to personal liberty.

13. _____ Ethical challenges primarily center upon the relationship one individual has with another individual.

## Multiple Choice

Select the best response.

1. Ethics is:

    A) Based on traditional religious teachings and moral habit

    B) The formal study of moral choices that conform to standards of conduct

    C) Principles of "right" conduct that an individual internalizes

    D) B and C

2. One looks to ethics:

    A) When the enforcement of law does not appear to bring justice

    B) When right behavior appears to bring about a wrong effect

    C) When personal sacrifice is the consequence of following ideals

    D) All of the above

3. The societies of two different countries may place different values on the role of women in the workplace. These different values would result in:

    A) Ethical conflict

    B) Values conflict

    C) Religious conflict

    D) Morals conflict

4. "Habitual truthfulness and honesty" is the definition of:

   A) Ethics

   B) Veracity

   C) Privacy

   D) All of the above

5. Systematic statements of principles involved in dealing with ethical dilemmas are referred to as:

   A) Ethical behavior

   B) Ethical theories

   C) Ethical conflict

   D) A and C

6. The clash between an individual's selfish interests and his or her obligation to an organization is referred to as:

   A) Conflict of interest

   B) Moral conflict

   C) Religious conflict

   D) Values conflict

7. You have discussed with your supervisor a new idea that you feel would increase production. She tells you to "leave those decisions to the brains of the department." What ethical challenge would this fall under?

   A) Impaired employee

   B) Disparagement of employee

   C) Conflict of interest

   D) Moral dilemma

8. Consequentialism is also known as:

   A) Utilitarianism

   B) Deontology

   C) Moral consequences

   D) Ethical consequences

## Matching

Match the job titles in Column I to their descriptions in Column II.

|  | **Column I** |  | **Column II** |
|---|---|---|---|
| 1. _____ | Ethics | A. | The concepts that give meaning to an individual's life and serve as the framework for decision making. |
| 2. _____ | Morals | B. | The study of moral choices that conform to professional standards of conduct. |
| 3. _____ | Values | C. | The principles of how human beings relate to one another under certain circumstances. |
| 4. _____ | Etiquette | D. | A body of rules of action or conduct prescribed by a controlling authority that has binding legal force. |
| 5. _____ | Law | E. | The principles or fundamental standards of "right" conduct that an individual internalizes. |

## Short Answer

1. You are eating lunch in the hospital's cafeteria and a woman sits down next to you and starts to cry. She turns to you unexpectedly and tells you that her husband is dying and she has been asked to remove life support. You are vehemently opposed to withdrawing life support. What would you say to her?

_____

_____

_____

2. What are the three elements that make up the ethical concept of autonomy?

_____

_____

_____

3. Name the two main ethical theories, and briefly describe each one.

_____

_____

_____

_____

4. Why is it important for a group to formulate and adhere to a code of ethics?

_____

_____

5. What is the difference between a potential conflict of interest and an actual conflict of interest?

_____

_____

_____

6. What does serving as a role model mean? Provide examples.

_____

_____

## Case Exploration

1. Review the code of ethics of AHIMA, and then review a code of ethics of another health care association (see the Web sites listed at the end of Chapter 4). Compare the ways in which they are the same and the ways they are different. Discuss why they are different.

2. What are your own ideas about the relationship between values and ethics?

3. Select one of the following ethical issues about which to write (at minimum) a three-page paper. Include at least two articles from health care journals (not Web articles unless they are from a journal) as sources. Summarize the information you collect and provide your own reflections. Chapter 4 contains a brief discussion of each of the following:

   - Family planning
   - Contraception
   - Artificial insemination
   - In vitro fertilization
   - Surrogate mothers
   - Abortion
   - Perinatal ethics
   - Prenatal testing
   - Prenatal surgery
   - Eugenics
   - Gene therapy
   - Euthanasia
   - Sterilization
   - Organ transplants

## The StudyWARE™ Challenge

Using the StudyWARE on your student software CD-ROM, complete the following activities:

1. Study the flash cards for Chapter 4 to review the key terms in this chapter.

2. Solve the crossword puzzle for Chapter 4.

3. Complete the quiz in test mode for Chapter 4. Record your score in the space below, and print out your results for your instructor.

---

**StudyWARE Quiz Chapter 4**

Date Taken: _____

Score: _____

---

# CHAPTER 5

# Health Care Data Content and Structures

## Learning Objectives

1. Describe the categories of data collected and maintained by health care providers.

2. Summarize the uses and users of health care data.

3. Trace the development of the concept of the personal health record.

4. Explain the concept of data flow and describe three data flow approaches.

5. Compare and contrast the concepts of forms design and forms control, and explain their application to paper-based and electronic health records.

6. Define the terms *data storage, data retention,* and *data destruction,* and explain their relationship to a records management system.

7. Distinguish between the concepts of indices and registries, and identify multiple examples of each.

## Acronym Review

Write out the following acronyms.

1. PHR: _____

2. COD: _____

3. H&P: _____

4. MPI: _____

## Key Terms Review: Filing Systems

Match the filing systems in Column I to their descriptions in Column II.

| | Column I | | Column II |
|---|---|---|---|
| 1. _____ | Alphabetic | A. | Assigns patients in chronological order as the patient is admitted or readmitted to the same health care facility. |
| 2. _____ | Serial numbering | B. | Assigns new numbers to the same patient regardless of the number of times the patient is admitted or registered at the same health care facility. |
| 3. _____ | Serial unit numbering | C. | Arranges patient files in alphabetical order, with the surname first, the first name second, and the middle initial third. |
| 4. _____ | Unit numbering | D. | A patient is reassigned the same number that was assigned when the patient was initially registered or admitted to the health care facility. |

## True or False

Indicate whether the following statements are true (T) or false (F). If a statement is false, rewrite it to make it true.

1. _____ Administrative data includes consent for treatment, authorization for use, release of information, and advance directives.

   _____

2. _____ Clinical data are recorded by a variety of physicians, nurses, and allied health professionals.

   _____

3. _____ A written signature or a computer-generated signature cord is called "authorship."

   _____

4. _____ With regard to a source-oriented health record, the department that provided the data is the "source."

   _____

5. _____ In a source-oriented health record, data and forms are arranged in chronological order by the source or department.

   _____

6. _____ Documentation requirements are time consuming for the health care provider using the problem-oriented record.

   _____

7. _____ Each episode of care is separated into a different section of the record in an integrated record.

   _____

8. _____ If you want to compare similar information over time, the integrated record is the best to use.

   _____

9. _____ Quantitative analysis concentrates on what forms or data should be present in, but are missing from, the health record.

   _____

10. _____ Qualitative analysis involves assembling and analyzing the record for accuracy and completeness.

    _____

11. _____ Qualitative analysis of the health record concentrates on the quality of the record content and not the quality of the medical care rendered to the patient.

    _____

12. _____ Quantitative analysis focuses on requirements of statutory provisions, administrative regulations, accrediting standards, professional guidelines, and institutional standards.

    _____

13. _____ The health record is a communication tool for providers treating patients.

_____

14. _____ Public health officials use the data in the health record to monitor the overall health status of a population.

_____

15. _____ The data in a health record serves as the basis of evidence in adjudication of criminal and civil cases to reconstruct an episode of patient care.

_____

16. _____ Data in the health record are used by many to manage the costs of care, including managed-care entities that make appropriate pricing and cost estimates and health care organizations that contract with managed-care entities.

_____

17. _____ Quality of care cannot be indicated by data in a health record.

_____

18. _____ Data recorded at the time that patient care is rendered can serve as the basis for the review of quality patient care.

_____

19. _____ Patients need to know and understand data in order to direct their own care and make informed choices.

_____

20. _____ Data in health records can determine the appropriate use of taxpayer dollars.

_____

21. _____ Data in health records cannot be used to prove fraud; only financial records can be used.

_____

22. _____ Data found in the health record can help evaluate occupational hazards that may impede performance in the workplace.

_____

23. _____ A PHR is a collection of a patient's important health information that is actively maintained and updated in paper or electronic form by the patient.

_____

24. _____ A data flow diagram displays how data movement is tracked.

_____

25. _____ In unidirectional data flow, data move in a linear arrangement, crossing from one person to another without interruption.

_____

26. _____ Multidirectional data flow begins by moving data in a linear arrangement but changes by rearranging the data so that they return to the sender at some point and then continue toward the original linear path.

27. _____ Standards of accuracy, completion, and protection from unauthorized disclosure do not impact the flow of health information.

28. _____ Forms design focuses on determining the purpose, use, and users of a health care form.

29. _____ "Record identification system" refers to the wristbands that patients wear when hospitalized.

30. _____ Using a decentralized filing approach, all records created by the health care provider are stored in a single location.

31. _____ Alphabetic systems arrange patient files in alphabetical order, with the surname first, the first name second, and the middle initial third.

32. _____ Statutes of limitations affect retention policies.

33. _____ A record retention schedule should include microfilm/microfiche, magnetic tape, optical discs, or electronic systems, including archiving systems.

34. _____ HIPAA requires that covered entities retain records showing HIPAA compliance for a period of 10 years.

35. _____ Incident reports should be filed in a patient record.

## Multiple Choice

Select the best response.

1. Socioeconomic data such as patient name, address, date of birth, and next of kin are also referred to as:

    A) Clinical data

    B) Administrative data

    C) Discharge data

    D) Data

2. A patient's health and course of treatment and care is called:

   A) Clinical data

   B) Secondary data

   C) Discharge data

   D) Administrative data

3. The integrity of the health record depends on:

   A) Authorship, authentication, timeliness, and completeness

   B) Authentication, clinical documentation, and completeness

   C) Handwriting of provider, authorship, and authentication

   D) Problem-oriented, timeliness, and completeness

4. The strength of this type of medical record is that all data and forms related to the specific source or department are readily available for review:

   A) Clinical

   B) Source-oriented

   C) Problem-oriented

   D) Integrated

5. The health record that is organized by placing all of the patient's problems in context with one another is known as:

   A) Source-oriented

   B) Problem-oriented

   C) Problem-SOAP notes

   D) Integrated

6. The health record that uses an intermingled order for organization is:

   A) Source-oriented

   B) Integrated

   C) Problem-oriented

   D) Clinical

7. The health record can be used for:

   A) Legal purposes

   B) Quality of care

   C) Educational purposes

   D) All of the above

8. According to HIPAA, administrative data includes all of the following, except:

    A) Consent forms

    B) Test results

    C) Contact information for health care providers

    D) Billing and insurance information

9. Clinical data includes all of the following, except:

    A) Authorization for organ donation

    B) Eye and dental records

    C) Opinions of specialists

    D) Recent physical examination results

10. Data that are input into the health record by a clinician, processed by the health information management (HIM) professional, and later stored according to established standards and requirements are an example of this kind of data flow:

    A) Unidirectional

    B) Bidirectional

    C) Multidirectional

    D) B and C

11. As a result of the introduction of sophisticated computer systems and the implementation of other technology devices, the HIM professional's view of data changed. Data flow may begin as bidirectional but then rearranges data to send them to multiple locations, or it may begin by sending the data to multiple locations before the course of the data flow ends. What type of data flow is this?

    A) Unidirectional

    B) Bidirectional

    C) Multidirectional

    D) A and B

12. Which of the following addresses how data, once collected and displayed, must be maintained and made available to those users with a legitimate reason for access?

    A) Data storage

    B) Retention storage

    C) Form storage

    D) Electronic data exchange

13. The HIPAA Security Rule focuses on:

    A) Data integrity

    B) Access control

    C) Technical safeguards

    D) All of the above

## Matching: Clinical Data

Match the data in Column I to their descriptions in Column II.

|  | Column I |  | Column II |
|---|---|---|---|
| 1. _____ | History and physical | A. | Descriptions of treatments rendered and procedures performed, including findings and results. |
| 2. _____ | Clinical observation and progress | B. | A report of the patient's current and past history and findings of a physical examination. |
| 3. _____ | Reports of treatment and procedures | C. | A summary of the patient's stay in the acute care facility, including final diagnoses and prognosis. |
| 4. _____ | Consultation reports | D. | Reports and summaries by health care providers of the patient's illness and treatment, including a needs assessment and a plan of care. |
| 5. _____ | Discharge summary | E. | Reports of the patient's condition provided by a health care provider other than the attending physician. |

## Matching: Terms for Data Quality

Match the terms in Column I to their definitions in Column II.

|  | Column I |  | Column II |
|---|---|---|---|
| 1. _____ | Accuracy | A. | Each data element correlates in meaning to the collection purpose. |
| 2. _____ | Accessibility | B. | Required data items are all collected. |
| 3. _____ | Comprehensiveness | C. | Each data element has a clear meaning. |
| 4. _____ | Consistency | D. | Data are collected easily and legally. |
| 5. _____ | Currency | E. | Data are collected when necessary. |
| 6. _____ | Definition | F. | Values are correct and valid. |
| 7. _____ | Granularity | G. | Data values do not vary across applications. |
| 8. _____ | Precision | H. | Data values fall within acceptable ranges. |
| 9. _____ | Relevancy | I. | Data are up-to-date at time of collection. |
| 10. _____ | Timeliness | J. | Each data element is defined to the necessary level of detail. |

## Complete the Table

Identify the record retention guidelines set forth by AHIMA for the following:

| | |
|---|---|
| Diagnostic images | |
| Disease index | |
| Fetal heart monitor records | |
| Master patient/person index | |
| Operative index | |
| Patient health/medical records for adults | |
| Patient health/medical records for minors | |
| Physician index | |
| Register of births | |
| Register of deaths | |
| Register of surgical procedures | |

## Personal Health Record Activity

You are trying to help your friend complete her personal health record. You suggest separating the PHR contents into two groups: administrative and clinical. Determine whether the following types of data are administrative data (A) or clinical data (C).

_____ Personal identifiers such as name, date of birth, and Social Security number

_____ Immunization and allergy records

_____ Medication, exercise, and counseling records

_____ Billing and insurance information, including receipts

_____ Recent physical examinations results

_____ Authorization of organ donation

_____ Contact information in case of an emergency

_____ Living wills and advance directives

_____ Eye and dental records

_____ Consent to treat, release of information, and notice of privacy practices forms

_____ Opinions of specialists

_____ Correspondence between patient and health care provider

_____ Contact information for health care providers

_____ Personal and family history

## Short Answer

1. Differentiate between timeliness and completeness of a health record.

_____

_____

_____

2. List the four parts of SOAP notes.

_____

3. Discuss the differences between concurrent and retrospective analyses.

_____

_____

_____

_____

4. How does concurrent analysis help with the financial side of health care?

_____

_____

5. List five uses of clinical and/or nonclinical data.

_____

_____

_____

_____

6. List three possible internal uses for data from the health record.

_____

_____

_____

7. Discuss how the data in health records can support research.

_____

_____

8. Discuss how the personal health record benefits the health care of a patient.

_____

_____

_____

_____

_____

_____

_____

_____

9. Outline the multidirectional flow of information in an acute care facility.

_____

_____

_____

_____

_____

_____

_____

_____

10. In forms design, what is meant by uniformity and simplicity?

_____

_____

_____

_____

11. What are the differences between forms design for a paper record and for an electronic record?

_____

_____

_____

_____

_____

12. The retention and destruction of the health record are governed by more than HIPAA law. What are some of the other reasons or agencies that impact retention and storage?

_____

_____

13. You sit on a health record subcommittee on forms management. What are the four practices that should be followed?

_____

_____

_____

## Case Exploration

1. Your health care facility is in a flood zone area. As director of the department, you have been asked to develop a disaster plan that will protect the paper-based records that are used. Describe some options that you would investigate for a disaster plan.

2. You sit on the medical record committee that is exploring the option of moving from a paper-based record to an electronic record. Develop a handout to discuss at the next meeting that explains the differences between the paper-based record and the electronic record.

## The StudyWARE™ Challenge

Using the StudyWARE on your student software CD-ROM, complete the following activities:

1. Study the flash cards for Chapter 5 to review the key terms in this chapter.

2. Solve the hangman activities for Chapter 5.

3. Complete the quiz in test mode for Chapter 5. Record your score in the space below, and print out your results for your instructor.

| StudyWARE Quiz Chapter 5 |
| --- |
| Date Taken: _____ |
| Score: _____ |

## The DVD Hookup

Program 3: Health Services Organization and Delivery

Case 3.1: Preventable Death

During a quality improvement committee meeting, the HIM director, the quality improvement coordinator, and a physician discuss the death of a patient. If the physician had been able to access the patient's medical history, he or she would have known about the patient's drug allergy and chosen another drug. Even if a patient has a medical record at your facility, the medical record is not always immediately available—this is why the electronic health record is so valuable. The existence of a regional health information organization (RHIO) or a personal health record might have resulted in a different outcome.

## Case Discussion

1. What legal issues can you identify?

_____

_____

_____

_____

_____

_____

_____

_____

2. What could have prevented this death?

_____

_____

3. What role could electronic health records have played in this situation?

_____

_____

_____

4. What role could the PHR have played in this case?

_____

_____

_____

_____

5. What role could an RHIO have played in this case?

_____

_____

_____

# CHAPTER 6

# Nomenclatures and Classification Systems

## Learning Objectives

1. Differentiate between the terms *medical language, vocabulary,* and *nomenclature.*

2. List nomenclatures that are prominent in the health information management field.

3. Understand the goal of the Unified Medical Language System.

4. List and explain the three Knowledge Sources of the Unified Medical Language System.

5. Identify the major classification systems currently in use.

6. Understand how the introduction of the prospective payment system and diagnosis-related groups affected the health information management field.

7. Describe the concept of case mix management.

8. Identify the impact of technology upon the coding function.

## Acronym Review

Write out the following acronyms.

1. ABC codes: _____

2. CDT: _____

3. ICD-10: _____

4. ICF: _____

5. ICIDH: _____

6. CPT: _____

7. DSM-IV: _____

8. HCPCS: _____

9. SNDO: _____

10. SNOMED: _____

11. SNOP: _____

12. ICD: _____

13. ICD-O-3: _____

14. ICD-9-CM: _____

## Key Terms Review

Match the terms in Column I to their definitions in Column II.

|  | **Column I** |  | **Column II** |
|---|---|---|---|
| 1. _____ | Encoders | A. | The practice of selecting a code and submitting a bill for a higher level of reimbursement than actually rendered. |
| 2. _____ | Groupers | B. | The words, their pronunciation, and the methods of combining them that have been established by long periods of usage and are understood by the medical profession. |
| 3. _____ | Optimizing programs | C. | Groupings of similar items, such as diseases and procedures, that serve as a way to organize related entities for easy retrieval. |
| 4. _____ | Upcoding | D. | The first level of a decision tree to reach a diagnosis-related group (DRG), generally based on an organ or system. |
| 5. _____ | Major diagnostic category | E. | Software programs that use branching logic to arrive at the most accurate DRG. |
| 6. _____ | Eponyms | F. | Software tools that incorporate the text and logic of coding systems in an automated form. |
| 7. _____ | Medical language | G. | Software programs that seek the highest-paying DRG based on the codes assigned and in compliance with prevailing regulations. |
| 8. _____ | Nomenclature | H. | A systematic listing of proper names for concepts, items, actions, and other aspects of a particular area of interest or knowledge. |
| 9. _____ | Vocabulary | I. | Words based on the personal names of people. |
| 10. _____ | Classification systems | J. | A list of words or phrases and their associated meanings that have been accepted by a discipline, group, or organization to express, organize, and index the concepts and phenomena of interest. |

## True or False

Indicate whether the following statements are true (T) or false (F). If a statement is false, rewrite it to make it true.

1. _____ Clinical terminologies describe the medical care process in a standard manner.

_____

2. _____ The language of medicine forms the basis for the understanding and management of health information.

_____

3. _____ Medical language is necessary for providers to know, but health information managers do not need to know it since they deal with data only.

_____

4. _____ Natural language processing and auto-coding technologies are being developed so that diagnoses and procedure codes will assign codes at the point of care.

_____

5. _____ Changes brought on by technology will shift the roles of coders to oversight and quality assurance.

## Multiple Choice

Select the best response.

1. Words based on the personal names of people are also called:

    A) Eponyms

    B) Nomenclatures

    C) Vocabulary

    D) Terminology

2. The term that describes the vocabulary that specializes in words or phrases of a medical nature is:

    A) Clinical vocabulary

    B) Eponym

    C) Nomenclatures

    D) Clinical terminology

3. A recognized system of preferred clinical or medical terminology is also called:

    A) Nomenclature

    B) Clinical data

    C) Clinical terminology

    D) Eponym

4. Which of the following refers to the manner in which clinical data are presented using classification systems and clinical vocabulary?

    A) Clinical terminology representation

    B) Clinical data presentation

    C) Clinical data representation

    D) None of the above

5. Another term for data mapping is:

    A) Clinical data representation

    B) Clinical terminology representation

    C) Clinical vocabulary

    D) None of the above

6. Data mapping is a:

    A) Clinical coding system

    B) Linking system between a target and a source

    C) Natural language processor

    D) Presentation system

## Short Answer

1. What is the difference between medical language, vocabulary, and nomenclature? Give an example of each.

_____

_____

_____

_____

_____

_____

2. Name three nomenclatures used in the health information management field.

_____

_____

_____

3. Why is the concept of standardization important as it relates to health information management?

_____

_____

4. What is the purpose of the Unified Medical Language System?

_____

_____

_____

5. What are the purposes of the UMLS Metathesaurus, the SPECIALIST Lexicon, and the UMLS Semantic Network?

_____

_____

_____

6. How do classification systems differ from nomenclatures?

7. List several major classification systems in use today.

8. Besides reimbursement, what are other uses for DRGs?

9. How did PPS and DRGs change the field of health information management?

10. What does the term *case mix management* refer to?

11. Describe the impact of automation and technology on coding.

_____

_____

_____

## The StudyWARE™ Challenge

Using the StudyWARE on your student software CD-ROM, complete the following activities:

1. Study the flash cards for Chapter 6 to review the key terms in this chapter.

2 Solve the crossword puzzle for Chapter 6.

3 Complete the quiz in test mode for Chapter 6. Record your score in the space below, and print out your results for your instructor.

| |
|---|
| **StudyWARE Quiz Chapter 6** |
| Date Taken: _____ |
| Score: _____ |

## The DVD Hookup

Program 1: Health Data Management

Case 1.3: Transitioning to ICD-10-CM and ICD-10-PCS

A coder goes to see his supervisor to find out about planning the changeover to ICD-10-CM and ICD-10-PCS. Since coded data are so critical to the health care system, this is not a transition that can be handled lightly. Problems in the transition could result in problems with reimbursement, monitoring quality, research, strategic planning, fraud and abuse, and resource utilization. Problems from the transition could occur at the facility level and even at the national level. The HIM professional should be instrumental in this transition as a clinical data specialist.

## Case Discussion

1. Do you agree with the coding supervisor? Why or why not?

_____

_____

2. If you were the coding supervisor, how would you have responded?

_____

_____

_____

_____

3. If you were the coder, what would you have done?

_____

_____

4. What are some steps the coder could take to prepare?

_____

_____

5. Why should we convert to ICD-10-CM and ICD-10-PCS?

_____

_____

_____

Program 1: Health Data Management

Case 1.4: Encoder System Update

A coder visits the HIM director to file a complaint about her supervisor and the failure to ensure that the coding updates are loaded in a timely manner. Failure to update these codes will result in the assignment of invalid or incorrect codes. This is much more serious now that there is no longer a grace period for using the new codes. Reporting invalid or incorrect codes can result in a number of problems for the health care facility.

## Case Discussion

1. What impact could the delay in instituting the coding updates have on the coders?

_____

_____

_____

2. What impact could the delay in instituting the coding updates have on the organization?

_____

_____

_____

_____

_____

3. If you were the director, how would you handle the coding supervisor?

_____

_____

_____

_____

_____

4. What is poor data quality?

_____

_____

# CHAPTER 7

# Quality Health Care Management

## Learning Objectives

1. Trace the historical developments of data quality management, performance improvement, risk management, and utilization management.

2. Differentiate between the various approaches to quality in the health care context.

3. Explain the relationship between quality and health care.

4. Use quality analysis tools to display and interpret data effectively.

5. Understand the role of government and private initiatives to promote and utilize data to support quality initiatives.

6. Understand the concept of performance improvement, including benchmarking, the ORYX Initiative, and CATCH.

7. Define the terms *risk* and *risk management.*

8. Describe the utilization review process.

## Acronym Review

Write out the following acronyms.

1. CATCH: _____

2. PERT: _____

3. PSDA: _____

4. PSCA: _____

5. (D)MAIC: _____

6. AHRQ: _____

7. HCUP: _____

8. RHIO: _____

9. NHII: _____

10. NCQA: _____

11. HEDIS: _____

12. QI: _____

13. OASIS: _____

14. ERM: _____

15. TEFRA: _____

## Key Terms Review

Match the terms in Column I to their definitions in Column II.

|  | **Column I** |  | **Column II** |
|---|---|---|---|
| 1. _____ | Utilization review | A. | Determines if the admission and/or procedure/treatment plan is medically necessary and appropriate for the setting. |
| 2. _____ | Case management | B. | Continued-stay review; assures the continued medical necessity. |
| 3. _____ | Case managers/ utilization coordinators | C. | Clinical review of the appropriateness of admission and planned use of resources. |
| 4. _____ | Preadmission review | D. | Ongoing review of patient care in various health care settings. |
| 5. _____ | Admission review | E. | Process of coordinating the activities employed to facilitate the patient's release from the hospital. |
| 6. _____ | Concurrent review | F. | Performed at the time of admission. |
| 7. _____ | Discharge planning | G. | Nurses or health information managers with responsibility for managing the review process. |

## True or False

Indicate whether the following statements are true (T) or false (F). If a statement is false, rewrite it to make it true.

1. _____ Total quality management refers to the high grade, superiority, or excellence of data.

_____

2. _____ The patient health record is crucial to measuring patient care.

_____

3. _____ In Six Sigma, black belts are technical personnel who are trained to apply the statistically based methodology.

_____

4. _____ The Six Sigma Improvement Methodology, when applied, works toward correction of defects rather than the elimination of errors.

_____

5. _____ AHRQ is a scientific research agency located within the Public Health Service (PHS).

_____

6. _____ AHRQ focuses on quality of care research.

_____

7. _____ AHRQ is more focused on clinical practice than evidence-based guidelines.

_____

8. _____ A Pareto chart, sometimes referred to as a fishbone or Ishikawa diagram, identifies major categories of factors that influence an effect and the subfactors within each of those categories.

9. _____ Core measurements refer to changes or end results, whether positive or negative.

10. _____ Core measurements are a part of benchmarking.

11. _____ Benchmarking comes into play at the data assessment level.

12. _____ Nursing Home Compare focuses on 15 quality measures.

13. _____ The Nursing Home Compare report compares data from individual nursing homes against national and state averages.

14. _____ The OSCAR database is a comprehensive report that includes nursing home characteristics, citations issued during the three most recent state inspections, and recent complaint investigations.

15. _____ The Hospital Compare report currently reports on acute myocardial infarction, heart failure, pneumonia, and surgical infection prevention.

16. _____ One of the best practices for the prevention of infections after colon surgery is related to the timing of the administration of antibiotics and avoidance of prolonged administration of prophylaxis with antibiotics.

17. _____ The Home Health Quality Initiative report examines 10 quality measures related to outcome of care.

18. _____ MEDPAR is composed of data from the Medicare population that are reported from claims data submitted by health care facilities.

19. _____ Leapfroggroup.org uses data that are submitted voluntarily by health care organizations.

20. _____ Risk management is a clinical function focused on how to improve patient care.

21. _____ Benchmarking allows a health care agency to learn how a superior performer achieved its goals and to determine how to incorporate those methods into operational practice.

_____

22. _____ ORYX is the Joint Commission's performance improvement method.

_____

23. _____ Criteria are defined by the Joint Commission as the specifications against which performance or quality may be compared.

_____

24. _____ Risk management is a nonclinical function that focuses on how to reduce medical, financial, and legal risk to an organization.

_____

25. _____ The incident report is an integral component of any loss prevention program.

_____

26. _____ Risk managers often act as liaisons to a health care organization's attorneys.

_____

27. _____ The Health Insurance Portability and Accountability Act requires a covered entity to perform a risk analysis to determine security risks and implement standards to reduce risks and vulnerabilities to electronic protected health information.

_____

28. _____ A sentinel event is an unexpected occurrence involving death or serious physical or psychological injury.

_____

29. _____ Enterprise risk management includes the threat of terrorism and its impact on professionals, patients, and the community.

_____

30. _____ Utilization management includes prudent use of resources, appropriate treatment management, and early comprehensive discharge planning for continuation of care.

_____

31. _____ Post acute transfer policy is a part of the discharge planning process.

_____

32. _____ The Office of Inspector General is an important watchdog for PACT.

_____

## Multiple Choice

Select the best response.

1. The organization-wide approach to quality improvement is:

    A) Total quality management

    B) Continuous quality improvement

    C) Data quality

    D) A and B

2. The systematic, team-based approach to process and performance improvement is:

    A) Total quality management

    B) Continuous quality improvement

    C) Data quality

    D) A and B

3. Actions taken to establish, protect, promote, and improve the quality of health care are referred to as:

    A) Quality assurance

    B) Process improvement

    C) Performance improvement

    D) Quality management

4. Data errors can occur during many stages, including:

    A) The documentation process

    B) The abstracting process

    C) The coding process

    D) All of the above

5. Data errors can occur during many stages, including:

    A) The coding process

    B) The indexing and registry processes

    C) The interpreting process

    D) All of the above

6. The measurement of quality to a level of near perfection or without defects is defined as:

    A) Six Sigma

    B) PDCA

    C) FOCUS

    D) PDSA

7. The six steps of Six Sigma are included in:

    A) PDSA

    B) (D)MAIC

    C) PDCA

    D) FOCUS

8. The current organization that is based on the foundation that quality professionals in health care drive the delivery of vital data for effective decision making in health care systems is:

    A) NAHQ

    B) HEPIS

    C) CPHQ

    D) HAQAP

9. Assessment tools that can be used for quality processes include:

    A) Idea generation

    B) Data gathering and organizing techniques

    C) Cause analysis

    D) All of the above

10. Tools that can be used to analyze root causes include:

    A) Cause-and-effect diagrams

    B) Pareto charts

    C) PERT

    D) A and B only

11. A display tool that contains x- and y-axes and displays data proportionally is a:

    A) Histogram

    B) Bar graph

    C) Line graph

    D) Contrast chart

12. A graph that shows the relationship between two variables and is often used as the first step in regression analysis is a:

    A) Control chart

    B) Histogram

    C) Line graph

    D) Scatter diagram

13. The Home Health Outcome Assessment and Information Set is called:

    A) HEDIS

    B) OASIS

    C) JCAHO

    D) AHRQ

14. Fundamental to the concept of _____ is the review of a given process.

    A) Benchmarks

    B) Quality improvement

    C) Performance improvement

    D) Risk management

15. Reviews of health care records to determine if care provided to patients is essential for safety and quality of care, as well as reimbursement and compliance issues, are usually conducted by:

    A) Physicians

    B) Nurses

    C) Health information management professionals

    D) Information technology management

16. Examples of sentinel events that must be reviewed include:

    A) Significant adverse drug reactions and confirmed transfusion reactions

    B) Surgery on the wrong patient or body part

    C) Infant abduction or discharge of an infant to the wrong family

    D) All of the above

## Matching

Many tools are available to process and analyze data. Organizational tools include affinity diagrams, nominal group techniques, Gantt charts, and PERT.

Match the following organizational tools to their descriptions.

A. Nominal group technique

B. Gantt charts

C. PERT

_____ 1. Tool used to track activities according to a time sequence, thereby showing the interdependence of activities.

_____ 2. Tool for organizing ideas wherein a list of ideas is labeled alphabetically and then prioritized.

_____ 3. Graphic representations that show the time relationships in a project.

## Matching

Match the graphs to their definitions.

A.  Bar graph

B.  Histogram

C.  Pie chart

D.  Line graph

E.  Control chart

F.  Scatter diagram

_____ 1. Graph that shows the relationship between two variables and is often used as the first step in regression analysis.

_____ 2. Contains both the x- and y-axes, with the exception that it can display data proportionally.

_____ 3. Graph with statistically generated upper and lower control limits used to measure key processes over time.

_____ 4. Demonstrates the frequency of data through the use of horizontal and vertical axes.

_____ 5. Graph used to show relationships to the whole, or how each part contributes to the total product or process.

_____ 6. Lines to represent data in numerical form.

## Short Answer

1. The AHRQ is an important agency that contributes to quality health care. List the goals of the AHRQ.

_____

_____

_____

_____

_____

_____

2. Provide examples of health care improvement in the areas listed below.

| | |
|---|---|
| Safe | |
| Effective | |
| Patient-Centered | |
| Timely | |
| Efficient | |
| Equitable | |

3. Comment on the professional makeup of the NAHQ. How do these professionals impact QA?

_____

_____

_____

4. How are brainstorming and benchmarking used to address new ideas?

_____

_____

_____

5. What can place a health care facility on "accreditation watch"?

_____

_____

_____

6. Discuss the differences between basic risk management and enterprise risk management in health care.

_____

_____

_____

_____

_____

7. Discuss the TEFRA Act, covering diagnosis-related groups (DRGs) and the prospective payment system (PPS).

_____

_____

## Case Exploration

1. Choose one of the Hospital Quality Alliance measures listed in Table 7–6 that includes adult smoking cessation advice/counseling. Discuss with a classmate whether you feel this is an appropriate use of health care money.

2. The 10 steps for redesign are listed in Table 7–4. Comment on your understanding of each of the steps.

## Web Assignments

1. Five topics were addressed in Table 7–5. Using the NAHQ Web site (http://www.nahq.org), find three more topics that you feel are important *or* list three topics that are *not* listed that you feel should be.

2. Go to the AHRQ Web site (http://www.ahrq.gov). Summarize the various activities that are described on the Web site.

## The StudyWARE™ Challenge

Using the StudyWARE on your student software CD-ROM, complete the following activities:

1. Study the flash cards for Chapter 7 to review the key terms in this chapter.

2. Solve the hangman activities for Chapter 7.

3. Complete the quiz in test mode for Chapter 7. Record your score in the space below, and print out your results for your instructor.

---

**StudyWARE Quiz Chapter 7**

Date Taken: _____

Score: _____

---

## The DVD Hookup

Program 2: Health Statistics, Biomedical Research, and Quality Management

Case 2.2: Accurate and Timely Birth Certificate Reporting

The chief operations officer (COO) has an appointment with the HIM director to address a problem with the reporting of birth certificates to the state department of health. The problems include both data quality and turnaround time issues.

## Case Discussion

1. What might be causing the quality issues?

_____

_____

2. What steps should the HIM director take to rectify the backlog and quality issues?

_____

_____

_____

_____

_____

_____

3. There was a definite change in the demeanor of the COO between the time she arrived in the HIM director's office and when the meeting was over. What do you think caused the change?

_____

_____

4. What should be included in the plan the COO requested?

_____

_____

_____

Program 2: Health Statistics, Biomedical Research, and Quality Management

Case 2.3: Performance Measurement Reporting

The HIM director, chief information officer (CIO), nurse supervisor, COO, and quality improvement coordinator form a new committee to monitor the hospital's performance measurement processes and results reporting. The primary charge of the committee is to oversee the facility's efficient reporting of performance measurement cases to the Joint Commission and the Center of Medicare and Medicaid Services (CMS).

## Case Discussion

1. Can you think of some gaps that might exist in other departments? How could these be corrected?

_____

_____

_____

_____

_____

2. What tasks should be assigned, and what should be reviewed prior to the next meeting?

_____

_____

_____

_____

_____

_____

_____

3. Are the appropriate staff members involved?

_____

_____

_____

_____

4. How could the committee's meeting have been more efficient?

_____

_____

_____

# CHAPTER 8

# Database Management

## Learning Objectives

1. Define the terms *database* and *database management*.

2. Describe database design and its role in the information systems life cycle.

3. Trace the historical development of database management programs.

4. Explain the nature of data standards, particularly Health Level Seven as a messaging standard for hospital information systems.

5. Distinguish between the terms *clinical data repository, data warehouse, data mart,* and *data mining*.

6. Differentiate between the terms *data set, data element,* and *minimum data set*.

7. Identify the data sets most commonly used in health care institutions in the United States.

8. Trace the development of data exchange networks and identify efforts at the federal, state, and local levels to implement them.

## Acronym Review

Write out the following acronyms.

1. HIPDB: _____

2. MPI: _____

3. MEDPAR: _____

4. OLAP: _____

5. UACDS: _____

6. UHDDS: _____

7. MDS: _____

8. NPDB: _____

9. GUI: _____

10. SQL: _____

11. OQL: _____

12. SOM: _____

13. SDO: _____

14. ANSI: _____

15. WEDI: _____

16. HISB: _____

17. PMRI: _____

18. NEDSS: _____

19. NCVHS: _____

20. NHII: _____

21. DEEDS: _____

22. NPI: _____

23. EIN: _____

24. ONCHIT: _____

25. AHIC: _____

## Key Terms Review

Match the terms in Column I to their definitions in Column II.

| | Column I | | Column II |
|---|---|---|---|
| 1. _____ | Data | A. | Structured storage or collection of data. |
| 2. _____ | Information | B. | Process of linking terminology between two different schemes. |
| 3. _____ | Database | C. | Raw facts and figures. |
| 4. _____ | Data dictionary | D. | Standardized definitions of each data element. |
| 5. _____ | Data mapping | E. | Ability to manage a database so as to create, modify, delete, and view given data. |
| 6. _____ | Database management | F. | Knowledge resulting from the processing of data. |

## True or False

Indicate whether the following statements are true (T) or false (F). If a statement is false, rewrite it to make it true.

1. _____ Database management is central to the practice of health information management (HIM).

    _____

2. _____ Database design refers to a description of the logical and physical characteristics of an operational database.

    _____

3. _____ The database design specification provides the rationale for the decisions made during database design and relates them to the system or application requirements previously decided.

    _____

4. _____ Computer programmers and analysts write the programming code and supporting documentation for database design.

_____

5. _____ A data model is a representation of exactly what a database should exemplify to the end user.

_____

6. _____ "Yyyymmdd" is a data standard used to display a patient's date of birth.

_____

7. _____ ANSI is a profit organization that serves to accredit and coordinate the work of qualified groups that develop national standards within the private sector.

_____

8. _____ ANSI-HISB works on the standard electronic health record, coding, terminology, international data exchanges, and patient privacy.

_____

9. _____ An interface is a set of connected and communicating computers, devices, and software that support the delivery of patient care and the day-to-day business of health care.

_____

10. _____ An interface is the hardware or software necessary to connect the components of an information system together.

_____

11. _____ HL7 is an ANSI-accredited SDO that develops specifications that allow different health care software applications within an organization to communicate with one another.

_____

12. _____ ASC X12 is used for business transactions that include ordering, shipping, and invoicing products.

_____

13. _____ X12N deals with standards related to insurance and reimbursement by private third-party payers and government health care programs.

_____

14. _____ Health care providers must supply certain data via electronic means to facilitate claims processing.

_____

15. _____ A subset of a data warehouse is a data mart.

_____

16. _____ Data warehouses are less complex, easier to maintain, and less costly than data marts.

_____

17. _____ Data warehouses are a good source of data to be mined.

_____

18. _____ MPIs are sometimes viewed as data warehouses.

_____

19. _____ The UHDDS has applied to all short-term general hospitals treating patients enrolled in the Medicare and Medicaid programs.

_____

20. _____ Federal and state governments compare health care facility discharge data reported through UHDDS.

_____

21. _____ The UHDDS is applicable to long-term care settings.

_____

22. _____ The MDS operates in conjunction with Resident Assessment Protocols.

_____

23. _____ OASIS is a minimum data set applicable to home health settings.

_____

24. _____ The NPI is a nine-digit number—with a hyphen after the first two numbers—that is used as a Federal Employer Identifier.

_____

25. _____ The NPI identifier is to be used by hospitals, doctors, nursing homes, and other health care providers when filing claims electronically.

_____

## Multiple Choice

Select the best response.

1. The mechanism employed to track computer data elements, records, and files back to their antecedent user requirements is referred to as:

   A) Database design

   B) Database design specification

   C) Traceability

   D) Structured query

2. Which organization is commissioned by the U.S. Department of Health to reduce administrative costs by increasing electronic billing?

    A) ANSI

    B) HISB

    C) JCAHO

    D) WEDI

3. A method of electronic mail messaging that is conveyed between computers without manual intervention is called:

    A) Information system

    B) Interface

    C) Electronic data interchange

    D) Data standards

4. The electronic storage of data and information from individual patient medical records is:

    A) Clinical data repository

    B) Data warehouse

    C) Data mining

    D) Data mart

5. The process of finding unknown dependencies in large data sets using automated means is:

    A) Data mining

    B) OLAP

    C) Clinical data repository

    D) Data marts

## Short Answer

1. Explain the components of a data design specification.

| a. General Information | |
|---|---|
| b. Description | |
| c. Logical Characteristics | |
| d. Physical Characteristics | |

2. Describe the similarities and differences between entity-relationship data models and the semantic object model.

_____

_____

_____

_____

_____

_____

3. What are the four elements of the entity-relationship model? Discuss your understanding of the four elements.

_____

_____

_____

_____

4. Discuss skills that health information management professionals need to participate in database design.

_____

_____

_____

5. What are the differences among concurrency control, access control, and integrity control of database? Give an example for each one.

_____

_____

_____

_____

6. Discuss the importance of data standards in the health care community.

_____

_____

_____

7. Discuss the connection between data warehouses and online analytical processing.

_____

_____

_____

_____

_____

8. Review the list of common health care data sets found in Table 8–4. Comment on why these data sets contribute to health care.

_____

_____

_____

_____

## Case Exploration

1. You are asked to present an in-service to department directors on regional health information organizations. Develop a PowerPoint presentation to do so.

2. You are moving to an electronic health record. Prior to doing so, you want to decrease duplicate number errors in the MPI. How would you do that?

## The StudyWARE™ Challenge

Using the StudyWARE on your student software CD-ROM, complete the following activities:

1. Study the flash cards for Chapter 8 to review the key terms in this chapter.

2. Solve the crossword puzzle for Chapter 8.

3. Complete the quiz in test mode for Chapter 8. Record your score in the space below, and print out your results for your instructor.

| **StudyWARE Quiz Chapter 8** |
| --- |
| Date Taken: _____ |
| Score: _____ |

## The DVD Hookup

Program 4: Information Technology and Systems

Case 4.2: Data Quality Nightmare

The HIM director, chief information officer, and business office director meet to discuss problems with data quality in the hospital's records. In this scenario, the hospital has a problem with the data that it collects. The problems include how data are collected, inappropriately sized data fields, and inconsistent data element names.

## Case Discussion

1. What could have been done to prevent this situation?

_____

_____

_____

_____

2. What steps can they take to deal with consistency issues, duplicate records, and other challenges?

_____

_____

_____

_____

3. What are the characteristics of data quality?

_____

4. How can data quality be built into information systems?

_____

_____

_____

5. What are some problems that may arise as a result of poor data quality?

_____

_____

_____

_____

# CHAPTER 9

# Health Statistics

## Learning Objectives

1. Identify the representative types of statistics found in health care.

2. Understand the concepts involved in statistical literacy.

3. Distinguish between the measures of central tendency: mean, median, and mode.

4. Determine the appropriateness of a statistical instrument.

5. Recognize the different types of data and the sources from which data can be obtained.

6. Describe the typical formulae applied in health care settings.

7. Become familiar with the rate formula applied in health information management settings.

8. List the presentation methods used to communicate data in numerical form.

9. Outline the rules of construction that govern the creation of graphs.

10. Discern whether a graph is complete or incomplete.

11. Explain the value of productivity analysis and identify two methods.

## Acronyms Review

Write out the following acronyms.

1. NCHS: _____

2. CDC: _____

3. NVSS: _____

4. A&D: _____

5. A&C: _____

6. CTT: _____

7. DC: _____

8. DIS: _____

9. DD: _____

10. DIPC: _____

11. DOA: _____

12. IP: _____

13. IPSD: _____

14. LOS: _____

15. NB: _____

16. OB: _____

17. TRF-in: _____

## Key Terms Review

Match the terms in Column I to their definitions in Column II.

| | Column I | | Column II |
|---|---|---|---|
| 1. _____ | Statistics | A. | Subset or small part of a population. |
| 2. _____ | Census | B. | An entire group that has a common observable characteristic. |
| 3. _____ | Descriptive statistics | C. | The theoretical basis of statistics. |
| 4. _____ | Population | D. | The official counting of a population. |
| 5. _____ | Sample | E. | Data on human events. |
| 6. _____ | Inferential statistics | F. | Reaching conclusions based upon data from a sample. |
| 7. _____ | Applied statistics | G. | Statistics used to characterize or summarize a given population. |
| 8. _____ | Mathematical statistics | H. | The mathematics of the collection, organization, and interpretation of numerical data. |
| 9. _____ | Vital statistics | I. | Use of statistics and statistical theory in real-life situations. |

## Key Terms Review: Regression Analysis

Regression analysis is a statistical tool that is used to identify correlations between variables that were not otherwise obvious. There are several ways to use regression analysis. Match the terms in Column I to their definitions in Column II, so that you have the vocabulary to begin discussion of regression analysis.

| | Column I | | Column II |
|---|---|---|---|
| 1. _____ | Correlation | A. | Numerous variables are used to provide the answer. |
| 2. _____ | Predictive power | B. | Two variables will provide the answer. |
| 3. _____ | Simple regression/ univariate regression | C. | Can be used to solve a problem and predict the future outcome. |
| 4. _____ | Bivariate regression | D. | Mutual relation or interdependence between two or more things. |
| 5. _____ | Multivariate regression | E. | Only one variable will provide the answer. |
| 6. _____ | $R^2$ | F. | Most reveal a bell-shaped curve. |
| 7. _____ | Pearson product- moment correlation | G. | Used to determine whether a relationship exists between two variables when both variables are numbers. |
| 8. _____ | Bivariate regression | H. | Performed when a need exists to compare more than two groups. |
| 9. _____ | Pearson correlation | I. | Measures the relationship between two variables that are categorical. |

10. _____ Distributions

11. _____ ANOVA/*F*-test

12. _____ Chi-square

J.   Mathematical formula used to calculate the regression.

K.   A score that lies somewhere between 0 and 1.

L.   Can be a negative number or a positive number between –1 and 1.

## True or False

Indicate whether the following statements are true (T) or false (F). If a statement is false, rewrite it to make it true.

1. _____ Health care providers report data on deaths (mortality) on a routine basis to the state level.

_____

2. _____ Data on births are called natality.

_____

3. _____ Public health surveillance statistics commonly cover communicable diseases (e.g., AIDS and venereal diseases), child abuse, injuries caused by deadly weapons, and cancer.

_____

4. _____ There is special importance placed on the timeliness of reporting certain diseases from the local level to the federal level.

_____

5. _____ Rapid notification to the CDC is critical in light of the threat of bioterrorism in the United States today.

_____

6. _____ HIM practitioners are crucial members of the early response team.

_____

7. _____ Demographic statistics focus on the study of human populations, looking to the size of the populations and how they change over time.

_____

8. _____ Natality statistics are used in disease prevention and control and in planning community health care programs.

_____

9. _____ Measurements of central tendency are typical or representative of a set of data.

_____

10. _____ A mean is reached by adding together all of the scores in a distribution and dividing that total sum by the number of scores in the distribution.

_____

11. _____ The median is the value in the middle when all values are lined up in order of largest to smallest.

_____

12. _____ A mode is a score or number that occurs with the greatest infrequency.

   _____

13. _____ Standard deviation refers to the square root of a variance.

   _____

14. _____ Standard deviation tells how widely spread apart the values are within a set of data.

   _____

15. _____ A result is statistically significant if it is unlikely to have occurred by chance and the test condition being examined has no effect.

   _____

16. _____ The SPSS is a popular analytical software application.

   _____

17. _____ The process of having one computer application directly deposit data elements into a specialized data collection system is referred to as a cold feed process.

   _____

18. _____ The linking of procedure codes to charges is tracked using a computerized program known as a Charge Description Master (CDM).

   _____

19. _____ Diagnosis and procedure indices are used as source documents in statistical reporting for clinical needs.

   _____

20. _____ Incidence rates are the proportion of known cases of a disease for a particular time period divided by the total population for the same period.

   _____

21. _____ Incidence rates are the proportion of newly reported cases of a disease for a particular time period divided by the total population at risk during the same period.

   _____

22. _____ Mortality rates tell us the rate of death in a given population or community.

   _____

23. _____ A graph does not need to be self-explanatory because a written report accompanies it.

   _____

24. _____ Regression analysis is a fundamental element of grouper programs.

   _____

25. _____ Case mix refers to the types and volume of patients treated by a health care facility.

   _____

26. _____ Regression analysis is performed using millions of MEDPAR files in order to derive a high confidence level that the diagnosis-related group is measuring what it purports to measure.

27. _____ Most of the statistics collected in health information management departments are used for regression analysis.

28. _____ Descriptive statistics are collected and disseminated as needed by HIM.

29. _____ One of the roles of the HIM analyst is to determine whether existing cold data feeds are adequate.

30. _____ Labor analytics refers to the activity and business of determining whether a work area has enough staff.

31. _____ The importance of a control chart is to help a team determine whether a variation is normal or the result of special circumstances.

32. _____ An upward trend contains a section of data points that decrease over a time period, whereas a downward trend shows the opposite.

## Multiple Choice

Select the best response.

1. Bioterrorism events are tracked using public health:
   A) Mortality statistics
   B) Surveillance statistics
   C) Demographic statistics
   D) Morbidity statistics

2. Determining the rates of epidemiological statistics includes:
   A) Process control
   B) Reliability
   C) How data are collected
   D) All of the above

# Matching

Match the mathematical words in Column I to their definitions in Column II.

|  | **Column I** |  | **Column II** |
|---|---|---|---|
| 1. _____ | Percentage | A. | Two quantities being compared are of different units or kinds. |
| 2. _____ | Rounding | B. | Process of reducing the total of significant digits in a number. |
| 3. _____ | Ratio | C. | Specified amount in every hundred. |
| 4. _____ | Rate | D. | A part of an entire whole. |
| 5. _____ | Fraction | E. | Quantity that signifies the amount of one quantity relative to another. |

# Matching

Match the acronyms in Column I to their meanings in Column II.

|  | **Column I** |  | **Column II** |
|---|---|---|---|
| 1. _____ | DIPC | A. | Number of calendar days from the day of patient admission to the day of discharge. |
| 2. _____ | IPSD | B. | Number of patients present at the official census-taking time each day. |
| 3. _____ | LOS | C. | The total inpatient service days; the sum of all IPSD for each of the days of consideration. |
| 4. _____ | DIPC + IPSD | D. | Services received by one patient during one 24-hour period. |

# Matching

Match the graph terms in Column I to their definitions in Column II.

|  | **Column I** |  | **Column II** |
|---|---|---|---|
| 1. _____ | Bar graph | A. | Used to present the frequency of categorical data through the use of horizontal and vertical axes. |
| 2. _____ | Line graph | B. | Resembles a histogram except that it takes a line form rather than a bar form. |
| 3. _____ | Pie chart | C. | Vertical axis contains continuous intervals for categories. |
| 4. _____ | Histogram | D. | Represents the frequency of data through the use of a circle divided into sections. |
| 5. _____ | Frequency polygon | E. | Uses lines to represent data in numerical form. |

## Short Answer

1. Give the formulae for determining the following rates:

A. Occupancy rate: _____

B. Nosocomial infection rate: _____

C. C-section rate: _____

D. Autopsy rate: _____

2. Describe what each of these data refer to:

A. Discrete data: _____

B. Continuous data: _____

C. Categorical data: _____

D. Nominal data: _____

E. Ordinal data: _____

F. Interval data: _____

3. List the key elements in the notification process.

_____

_____

4. List the seven broad categories of patient data that are collected.

1. _____

2. _____

3. _____

4. _____

5. _____

6. _____

7. _____

5. Why are these data elements important?

_____

_____

_____

6. When morbidity rates are measured, what is being determined?

_____

7. You are new at displaying data in a graph. What are four graphing rules?

_____

_____

_____

_____

8. Discuss how labor analytics are used in HIM.

_____

_____

_____

_____

9. Control charts can have Type I and Type II errors. What does this mean?

_____

_____

_____

## Web Assignments

1. Define the following terms, then read the instructions below for a Web assignment.

_T_-test: _____

_____

Null hypothesis: _____

Go to the FORE at AHIMA Web site (http://www.ahima.org) and search for an article on a research study that uses the reliability, validity, conceptualization, and operationalization concepts described in Table 9–5; evaluate the article.

2. Go to either the U.S. Public Health Web site or your state's Department of Health Web site and find a study that collects aggregate data (e.g., a cancer surveillance study). Discuss how the data are used to identify specific areas that demonstrate a high percentage of problems or issues.

3. Go to health care Web sites (e.g., AHRQ, AHIMA, HIMSS) and search for a research article that uses regression analysis. Explain the analysis in "layman's terms." Discuss how you can enhance your skills in this area.

## The StudyWARE™ Challenge

Using the StudyWARE on your student software CD-ROM, complete the following activities:

1. Study the flash cards for Chapter 9 to review the key terms in this chapter.

2. Solve the hangman activities for Chapter 9.

3. Complete the quiz in test mode for Chapter 9. Record your score in the space below, and print out your results for your instructor.

| |
|---|
| **StudyWARE Quiz Chapter 9** |
| Date Taken: _____ |
| Score: _____ |

## The DVD Hookup

Program 1: Health Data Management

Case 1.1: The Missing H&P Reports

The quality improvement (QI) coordinator has called a meeting with the HIM director, nurse supervisor, and chief of surgery to discuss the issue of missing History and Physical (H&P) reports prior to surgery and the loss of revenue that results from the cancellation of surgery due to the missing reports. The QI coordinator suggests that, in order to obtain a better understanding of the process and problems, a focus study be conducted to trend incidences by physician and transcriptionist.

## Case Discussion

1. What steps can this committee take to implement a quality improvement study?

_____

_____

_____

_____

_____

_____

_____

2. What types of reports and data should be analyzed as part of a quality improvement study?

_____

_____

3. How might the results of the study be presented when the full committee meets again?

_____

_____

4. Was the meeting handled appropriately?

_____

_____

_____

_____

_____

# CHAPTER 10

# Research

## Learning Objectives

1. Trace the development of research over time.

2. Compare and contrast qualitative and quantitative research methods.

3. Describe various types of research studies.

4. List the steps involved in research study design.

5. Understand the role that institutional review boards play in protecting human subjects involved in research studies.

6. Understand the role that institutional animal care and use committees play in protecting animal subjects involved in research studies.

7. Describe the emerging trends associated with protecting human subjects or animals used in research.

8. Trace the development of the epidemiology field over time.

9. Understand the basics of epidemiology, including the relationships among the agent, host, and environment in the progression of disease.

10. Compare and contrast descriptive, analytic, and experimental epidemiology.

## Acronym Review

Write out the following acronyms.

1. SBR: _____

2. IRB: _____

3. OHRP: _____

4. PHI: _____

5. DSMP: _____

6. DSMB: _____

7. IACUC: _____

## Key Terms Review

Match the elements of epidemiology in Column I to their definitions in Column II.

|       | Column I |     | Column II |
|-------|----------|-----|-----------|
| 1. _____ | Risk | A. | Living being upon whom the agent acts. |
| 2. _____ | Risk factors | B. | Suggests actions to be taken that will prevent healthy populations from developing a given disease. |
| 3. _____ | Relative risk ratio | C. | Factor that causes a disease. |
| 4. _____ | Primary prevention | D. | Agent capable of transmitting a pathogen. |
| 5. _____ | Secondary prevention | E. | Probability of an unfavorable event occurring. |
| 6. _____ | Tertiary prevention | F. | Limiting the level of disability and increasing the probability of rehabilitation for persons in an advanced stage of disease. |
| 7. _____ | Agent | G. | Factors that are associated with or increase the risk of acquiring a disease. |
| 8. _____ | Host | H. | Aggregate of the things, conditions, or influences surrounding the host. |
| 9. _____ | Environment | I. | Estimate of how much the risk of acquiring a disease increases with an individual's exposure. |
| 10. _____ | Vector | J. | Preclinical and clinical stages of disease intervention techniques. |

## True or False

Indicate whether the following statements are true (T) or false (F). If a statement is false, rewrite it to make it true.

1. _____ The scientific method refers to the process of discovery by systematic investigation.

   _____

2. _____ Qualitative research refers to the methodology that relies upon generating descriptive theory from data gleaned from an investigation.

   _____

3. _____ Research using the quantitative research method develops hypotheses that may be vague or general within a broad topic.

   _____

4. _____ Quantitative research methodology relies upon testing theories to make predictions.

   _____

5. _____ Qualitative research on the personal experiences and actions of those at risk of developing HIV or AIDS was important to containing the spread of the epidemic.

   _____

6. _____ The Food and Drug Administration requires satisfactory completion of clinical trials before a new treatment is made available to the public.

_____

7. _____ Efficiency in clinical trials refers to the benefits that accrue to the individual receiving care.

_____

8. _____ In clinical trials, efficiency refers to the resources consumed by the treatment.

_____

9. _____ In a controlled clinical trial, a placebo is something that resembles the treatment being studied but is substituted with a different treatment.

_____

10. _____ SBR studies focus on research dealing with human attitudes, beliefs, and behaviors.

_____

11. _____ A hypothesis rationale demonstrates why a certain study should be performed.

_____

12. _____ Methods used by the researcher follow the study rationale.

_____

13. _____ The OHRP administers the federal regulations that govern research involving human subjects.

_____

14. _____ De-identified data for research use are less restrictive than limited data.

_____

15. _____ HIPAA regulations offer two exceptions to IRB review: the use of de-identified data or a limited data set.

_____

16. _____ DSMPs and DSMBs serve to evaluate study data to ensure participant safety and study integrity.

_____

17. _____ DSMPs are mechanisms used by the study investigators, with information reported to the IRB.

_____

18. _____ A DSMB reviews and evaluates data gained from the research to ensure participant safety and study integrity.

_____

19. _____ At least one member of an IACUC must be a veterinarian.

_____

20. _____ The National Institutes of Health regulatory requirements include a provision for assurance that animal research supported by the NIH meets acceptable standards of care, use, and treatment.

_____

21. _____ Once a research team is funded by the NIH, it no longer needs to protect human subjects in clinical trails.

_____

22. _____ Epidemiology is the study of how and why diseases occur in different groups of human beings.

_____

23. _____ The underlying premise of epidemiology is that disease is present or absent due to certain characteristics that may be identified though study.

_____

24. _____ Nutrition and hygiene education, plus specific protective measures (e.g., immunizations and sanitation), are examples of tertiary prevention measures.

_____

25. _____ Limiting the level of disability and increasing the probability of rehabilitation for persons in an advanced stage of disease or disability is primary prevention.

_____

## Multiple Choice

Select the best response.

1. Research that is considered abstract and general, seeking to generate knowledge for knowledge's sake, is:

    A) Applied

    B) Laboratory

    C) Pure

    D) Experimental

2. The scientific method:

    A) Is a formal process

    B) Is an informal process

    C) Does not encourage generalizable knowledge

    D) Is done only in medicine

3. Research that is performed in the real world, where control over variables may be difficult, is:

    A) Pure

    B) Experimental

    C) Clinical

    D) Laboratory

4. Quantitative research:

   A) Emphasizes how a participant in a given setting constructs the world around herself

   B) Involves data that are contained in context

   C) Involves data that have the potential for revealing complexities

   D) Emphasizes the answer to a specific research quota

5. In qualitative research:

   A) Data have the potential for revealing complexities

   B) Established facts are important

   C) Defined models and detailed operations are used

   D) B and C

6. What is true about quantitative research?

   A) Variables may be manipulated and measured

   B) An element of control is present

   C) Randomization is used

   D) All of the above

7. Data aggregation studies:

   A) Use data from large numbers of medical records

   B) Focus on direct patient contact

   C) Use data from a small number of patient interviews

   D) Are general in nature

8. Obtaining informed consent and respecting the privacy of research subjects derive from the principle of:

   A) Respect

   B) Beneficence

   C) Justice

   D) All of the above

9. Requirements for studies to seek a balance between benefits and risks to the patient, along with strong research design that maximizes benefits and reduces harms, derive from which principle?

   A) Respect

   B) Risk

   C) Beneficence

   D) Ethics

## Matching

Match the categories of research in Column I to their definitions in Column II.

| | Column I | | Column II |
|---|---|---|---|
| 1. _____ | Pure | A. | Designed to answer a practical question. |
| 2. _____ | Applied | B. | Performed in the real world. |
| 3. _____ | Experimental research | C. | Uses variables, control, and randomization in an experiment. |
| 4. _____ | Descriptive research | D. | Seeking to generate knowledge for knowledge's sake. |
| 5. _____ | Clinical | E. | Description of individuals, groups, or situations. |
| 6. _____ | Laboratory | F. | Performed in a setting under tight control. |

## Complete the Table

Components of epidemiological inquiry:

| Title | Descriptive | Analytic | Experimental |
|---|---|---|---|
| Studies | _____ _____ | _____ _____ | _____ _____ |
| Focus | _____ _____ | _____ _____ | _____ _____ |

## Short Answer

1. What are the steps in research design?

_____

_____

_____

_____

_____

2. Describe the differences between research and research methodology.

_____

_____

_____

_____

_____

3. What are the differences between blind and double-blind studies?

_____

_____

_____

_____

4. What are the three types of IRB reviews that are allowed under federal regulations? Discuss the key components of each, and why there are differences in the review process.

_____

5. What is the IACUC, where is it usually located, and why is it important?

_____

_____

_____

_____

6. Why would a health information management (HIM) practitioner be a good fit as a research information manager?

_____

_____

_____

7. How do epidemiology and HIM intersect?

_____

_____

_____

_____

_____

_____

8. What are the differences between epidemics and pandemics?

_____

_____

_____

## Case Exploration

1. Review the discussions on research study process. Determine an area of HIM that you would like to research. Following the steps of research design, describe the process needed to conduct that specific research. Determine whether you would use quantitative or qualitative design.

2. Discuss medical research abuses of the middle and late 20th century. What impact has this had on human research today?

3. Epidemiology is essential to public health. Given the discussion about epidemic flu outbreaks, why are the epidemiology objectives listed in Table 10-10 important?

4. Review Table 10-11. Discuss any "surprises" you found in the comparison of the years 1900 and 2000 with regard to the predominant causes of death in the United States.

## Web Assignments

1. Go online and find an article on the use of clinical trails for the approval of drugs. Discuss the process reported in the article.

2. Search the Web for information on the Nuremberg Code. Are trials conducted in our current time frame related to war crimes?

3. Go to the Web site of the World Health Organization (http://www.who.int) and find the Declaration of Helsinki. Discuss the components of this declaration.

4. Go to the Web site of the National Commission (http://ohsr.od.nih.gov/guidelines/belmont.html) for the Protection of Human Subjects in Biomedical and Behavioral Research and review the components of the Belmont Report. Discuss the meaning of the key elements: (1) respect for persons, (2) beneficence, and (3) justice.

## The StudyWARE™ Challenge

Using the StudyWARE on your student software CD-ROM, complete the following activities:

1. Study the flash cards for Chapter 10 to review the key terms in this chapter.

2. Solve the crossword puzzle for Chapter 10.

3. Complete the quiz in test mode for Chapter 10. Record your score in the space below, and print out your results for your instructor.

---

**StudyWARE Quiz Chapter 10**

Date Taken: _____

Score: _____

---

## The DVD Hookup

Program 2: Health Statistics, Biomedical Research, and Quality Management

Case 2.1: How Can HIM Assist in Research Studies?

The HIM director gets a visit from a physician, one of the hospital's researchers, to ask about an upcoming therapeutic drug trial. Although most HIM professionals are not researchers, there are many ways that the HIM professional can be a valuable part of the research team. The knowledge that the HIM professional has on data collection, data quality, forms design, databases, data analysis, statistics, ethics, informed consent, and privacy and security make him or her an invaluable resource.

## Case Discussion

1. What are some ways in which the HIM staff member can assist a physician in conducting a research study?

2. What impact would HIPAA have on this process?

3. Are HIM departments typically involved in planning clinical trials?

4. How could the HIM director prepare for the meeting?

# CHAPTER 11

# Management Organization

## Learning Objectives

1. Understand the general principles of management: planning, organizing, directing, controlling, and leading.

2. Compare and contrast strategic planning with managerial, operational, and disaster planning.

3. Explain the interrelationships between planning, organizing, directing, controlling, and leading.

4. Describe the role that the leading function plays within an organization.

5. Trace the development of management theories over time.

6. Compare and contrast specialized management theories.

## Acronym Review

Write out the following acronyms.

1. MBO: _____

2. PERT: _____

3. ADA: _____

4. OSHA: _____

5. TQM: _____

6. PM: _____

7. KMS: _____

## Key Terms Review

Match the terms in Column I to their definitions in Column II.

|  | Column I |  | Column II |
|---|---|---|---|
| 1. _____ | Job | A. | Tool used in organizing work. |
| 2. _____ | Job analysis | B. | Tasks and responsibilities that are regarded as the regular assignments of an individual. |
| 3. _____ | Job evaluation | C. | Series of interrelated steps used to give standardization to routine tasks. |
| 4. _____ | Job description | D. | Compares tasks within jobs to one another. |
| 5. _____ | Work distribution chart | E. | Determines the content of a job. |
| 6. _____ | Procedures | F. | Written statement summarizing what an employee does. |

## Key Terms Review

Match the knowledge management terms in Column I to their definitions in Column II.

| | Column I | | Column II |
|---|---|---|---|
| 1. _____ | Knowledge | A. | Personal knowledge, or that knowledge contained in people's heads. |
| 2. _____ | Signals | B. | Ability to judge matters soundly. |
| 3. _____ | Data | C. | Understanding and use of a range of information. |
| 4. _____ | Information | D. | Raw facts and figures. |
| 5. _____ | Wisdom | E. | Can be recorded, archived, codified, or embedded into products. |
| 6. _____ | Explicit knowledge | F. | Organized and classified data put into context. |
| 7. _____ | Tacit knowledge | G. | Objects serving to convey data. |

## True or False

Indicate whether the following statements are true (T) or false (F). If a statement is false, rewrite it to make it true.

1. _____ Prioritization of processes and operations is the most significant step in a disaster recovery plan.

   _____

2. _____ Ranking will allow managers to determine the minimum number of staff necessary to perform each ranked function in priority order in a disaster.

   _____

3. _____ In disaster recovery, the organization as a whole assigns responsibilities to individuals and teams to coordinate the recovery process.

   _____

4. _____ Unpredictable and sometimes unpreventable hazards might endanger a disaster plan operation or survival.

   _____

5. _____ It is not necessary to test a recovery plan.

   _____

6. _____ Full-interruption testing is costly but often a first choice for managers planning disaster recovery.

   _____

7. _____ A created mechanism for comparing the progress of a project at different points in time is PERT.

   _____

8. _____ A Gantt chart is defined as a graphic representation of the time relationships in a project.

   _____

9. _____ PERT is the outgrowth of work performed by the U.S. Army to reduce the time frame projected to complete the Polaris Ballistic Missile Project.

_____

10. _____ PERT is particularly applicable to projects that have multiple variables.

_____

11. _____ PERT tracks activities according to a time sequence.

_____

12. _____ A PERT network differs from a Gantt chart in that it shows the interdependence between activities.

_____

13. _____ On a Gantt chart, the longest sequence of events to be completed will have the largest effect upon the project.

_____

14. _____ Product structure divides work and responsibilities around the characteristics of an organization's customers or markets.

_____

15. _____ An organization chart maps how positions within a department or organization are tied together along the principal lines of authority.

_____

16. _____ Informal and informational relationships present in organizations are part of an organization chart.

_____

17. _____ Ergonomics is the design of products, processes, and systems to meet the requirements and capacities of those people who use them.

_____

18. _____ Directing is the continuous process of decision making, instructing others, and giving orders.

_____

19. _____ Decision making is the act of reaching a conclusion.

_____

20. _____ Delegating means to entrust another person with selected powers and functions.

_____

21. _____ Work simplification is a method used to find easier and better ways of doing work.

_____

22. _____ Work simplification is designed to speed up work.

_____

23. _____ Controlling means activities are accomplished as planned and significant deviations from the plan are corrected.

_____

24. _____ Controlling is the least critical function in management.

_____

25. _____ Correcting problems in quality and quantities may result in changing standards.

_____

26. _____ Personal power rests on the authority inherent in the job status, title, or rank.

_____

27. _____ Personal power rests on the positive regard that others accord an individual.

_____

28. _____ Positional power emphasizes perception and belief.

_____

29. _____ Maslow's hierarchy of needs theory is a motivation theory.

_____

30. _____ Job satisfaction and job performance are separate concepts.

_____

31. _____ Maintenance factors are tied closely to the nature of the work itself.

_____

32. _____ Conflict is a usual occurrence in an organization.

_____

33. _____ Functional conflict can occur when personality differences cause conflicts among teams or groups.

_____

34. _____ Theory Y holds that the average employee dislikes work.

_____

35. _____ In Theory X, managers use fear as a motivator for workers.

_____

36. _____ In Theory Y, employees experience satisfaction as they contribute to the achievement of objectives.

_____

37. _____ Theory Z holds that responsibilities sought by employees are culturally related.

_____

38. _____ In Theory Z, employees are capable of self-control.

_____

39. _____ Process improvement refers to the efforts to implement changes to business processes as a means to improve performance.

_____

40. _____ Using the five "why"s method, the root causes of a problem are discovered by asking the question "why" at least four times in a given discussion.

_____

41. _____ Nominal group technique is particularly appropriate for large groups who wish to participate in the decision-making process or for long lists that require separation between vital and trivial ideas or items.

_____

42. _____ Multivoting is more appropriate for smaller groups or smaller lists of ideas or items.

_____

43. _____ Force field analysis is a tool applicable to identifying and visualizing the relationships of significant influencing forces.

_____

44. _____ A flowchart uses geometric symbols to show the steps in a sequence of operations.

_____

45. _____ An affinity diagram shows the relationship between factors in a problem.

_____

46. _____ An affinity diagram is the same as a fishbone diagram.

_____

47. _____ The Pareto principle posits that 20 percent of problems pose 80 percent of the impact.

_____

48. _____ The Pareto principle posits that 80 percent of problems pose 20 percent of the impact.

_____

## Multiple Choice

Select the best response.

1. Management:

   A) Is a process generally defined to include planning, organizing, directing, controlling, and leading

   B) Requires resources both external and internal to the manager

   C) Must meet objectives, attain goals, and produce results

   D) All of the above

2. In a broad sense, planning:

   A) Refers to those activities that outline what needs to be done

   B) Refers to how to accomplish what needs to be done

   C) Results in better use of both time and money

   D) All of the above

3. A risk assessment is:

   A) A method to measure an organization's level of preparedness to prevent a disaster

   B) A method to measure an organizations level of preparedness to recover from a disaster

   C) A comprehensive plan of actions to be taken

   D) A and B

4. What does not need to be done to plan for off-premise facility operations in a disaster?

   A) Prioritization of processes and operations

   B) Determine critical functions, procedures, and equipment

   C) Rank functions in priority order

   D) Prepare a detailed budget to carry out the plan

5. Gantt charts are applicable to all but which of the following projects?

   A) Projects in which the steps involved are highly interdependent

   B) Projects that pose limited changes to the process

   C) Projects that involve simple, repetitive tasks

   D) Projects that require simple and direct communication

6. What requires the most attention from a manager with respect to a PERT network?

   A) Showing interdependence between activities

   B) Looking for critical paths

   C) Tracking activities

   D) Comparing to the Gantt chart

7. Using work simplification, a manager looks at:

   A) Overtime usage

   B) Streamlining processes

   C) Unfinished work

   D) All of the above

8. Managers perform the controlling function in all but which of the following ways?

    A) Identifying the types of controls to be used

    B) Setting standards

    C) Planning objectives

    D) Monitoring performance

9. Quality of work can be measured by:

    A) Incident reports

    B) Spot-checking

    C) Budget

    D) A and B

10. The legitimacy principle of negotiation focuses on:

    A) Respect for the persons involved

    B) The fairness aspect

    C) Seeking the positions of those involved

    D) What is really sought by parties

11. Scientific management is credited to the work of many researchers. Which of the following researchers was not involved in this area of research?

    A) Frederick Taylor

    B) Abraham Maslow

    C) Henry Gantt

    D) Lillian Gilbreth

12. The basis of the work of Max Weber and other classical management theorists was that:

    A) Managers are expected to make all of the decisions

    B) Workers are cogs in a wheel

    C) Workers are functional

    D) All of the above

13. Humanistic management focuses on:

    A) Social relationships at work

    B) Managers working with and through people

    C) Managers being expected to make all decisions

    D) A and B

14. The behavioral scientists known for participatory management are:

    A) McGregor and Drucker

    B) Drucker and Gantt

    C) Weber and Hawthorne

    D) McGregor and Hawthorne

15. The theorists who introduced TQM were:

    A) Deming, Shewhart, Juran, and Ishikawa

    B) Gantt, Hawthorne, Mayo, and Drucker

    C) Drucker, McGregor, Deming, and Juran

    D) All of the above

16. Change management includes:

    A) Large-scale change

    B) Focusing on a change in human performance

    C) The use of Theory X as a model

    D) A and B

17. Process improvement has been shown to increase:

    A) Speed

    B) Productivity

    C) Profitability of organizations

    D) All of the above

18. Which of the following organizes information into a visual pattern to show the relationship between factors in a problem?

    A) Force field analysis

    B) Affinity diagram

    C) Cause and effect

    D) Fishbone analysis

## Matching

Match the planning tools in Column I to their definitions in Column II.

| | Column I | | Column II |
|---|---|---|---|
| 1. _____ | Policy | A. | Comprehensive written statement of consistent actions to be taken before, during, and after a disaster. |
| 2. _____ | Procedure | B. | An unanticipated event or condition, such as the implementation of a new and unexpected policy change, an adjustment to an emergency, or the realization of an aspect of strategic planning. |

3. _____    Operational planning

C.   A method used to measure an organization's level of preparedness to prevent and recover from a disaster.

4. _____    Disaster planning

D.   Decision-making guide that establishes the parameters for taking action and meeting objectives.

5. _____    Disaster recovery plan

E.   Series of interrelated steps that are documented and used to give standardization to routine tasks or structured problems.

6. _____    Risk assessment

F.   Focuses on how to minimize the effect that disruptions or destructions may have on organizations.

## Select All That Apply

Read the questions below and place an X next to the correct answers in the lists that follow.

1. Which of the following are good tests of a recovery plan?

_____ Simulate a disaster during nonbusiness hours.

_____ Employ parallel site testing.

_____ Make a checklist of essential elements in the plan against reality.

_____ Conduct a structured walk-through with those who will manage the recovery.

_____ Purposefully disrupt an organization's operations for a short time.

2. The function of organizing:

_____ Brings together resources in an orderly manner.

_____ Arranges resources in an acceptable fashion for goals and objectives to be achieved.

_____ Focuses on employee satisfaction.

_____ Focuses on the people involved.

_____ Focuses on the quality of work performed.

_____ Focuses on the procedures used in performing work.

_____ Focuses on the environment in which the work is performed.

3. Communication involves:

_____ Knowing who needs what information.

_____ A scientific management approach.

_____ Choosing an appropriate medium for disseminating information.

_____ Listening effectively.

_____ Conducting conflict resolution in a concise and timely way.

_____ Helping others to communicate effectively.

## Short Answer

1. The functions of project manager include:

_____

_____

_____

_____

_____

2. Why is it important to test a recovery plan?

_____

_____

_____

_____

3. You are the HIPAA Security Officer at your facility. What is your role in disaster recovery?

The HIPPA Security Officer is responsible for the information systems and various business operations in the event of a disaster; deciding what information systems, protected health information, and business functions are involved; and deciding when to invoke the disaster recovery plan.

_____

_____

_____

The health care manager must use the principles of organizational design to design a structure that will assist the organization to survive business cycles, respond to customer needs, and grow and thrive.

5. What are the steps to work simplification?

_____

_____

_____

_____

_____

6. How is the control function linked to performance evaluation of an employee?

_____

_____

7. What is the difference between the functions of leading and leadership?

_____

_____

_____

_____

8. What is the two-factor theory? Who designed it?

_____

_____

_____

9. What are the motivators that make a person stay at a job?

_____

_____

10. Principled negotiation includes seven factors. What are they?

_____

_____

11. What are the differences between knowledge management and a knowledge management system?

_____

_____

_____

_____

## Case Exploration

1. As director of health information management (HIM) in a long-term care center located in a flood zone, you are asked to develop a plan for disaster preparedness and recovery. Discuss the components that you will need to include in the plan.

2. As the manager of a home health care HIM department, you are developing telecommuting positions for coders. You need to make some decisions about the type of office furniture that will be ergonomically safe. Discuss the decision-making process you will need to go through.

3. Looking at your budget, you see that the cancer registry area has been increasing overtime for the last six months. You approach the supervisor of that area and ask her to look at ways to make changes to reduce overtime. She is a new supervisor, so you need to train her in the work simplification process. What will you ask her to do specifically with regard to the function of cancer registry?

4. You suspect that the release-of-information employee is releasing protected health information (PHI) without the proper patient release. What audit steps would you take to evaluate this?

5. You are trying to determine the quality and quantity of work done by employees who are responsible for scanning and indexing. There have been complaints by clinical staff that history and physical reports are not indexed to the same area of the electronic record. How would you evaluate this?

6. You have a long-term employee who has worked with the organization as it changed from a paper-based record system to an electronic one. The employee has mentioned that as a result of this change, the job is not as satisfying. Because you do not want the employee to leave, you employ some environmental techniques. What are they, and why you do think they will work?

7. Discuss examples of functional or dysfunctional conflict that you have experienced. Which of the conflict resolutions options have you used? Refer to Table 11–6.

8. Many who find change difficult will go through the stages of denial, resistance, bargaining, and depression before they reach the stage of acceptance. Reflect on how change affects you and whether these stages apply. Give an example.

9. You have been asked to lead a project on new strategies in quality management that will include professionals from information technology (IT), nursing, medical staff, and many other health departments. How will you approach this as a project manager?

10. You work in the IT department as an RHIA with a project assignment that will need input from a large group of people. You will be working with groups of 15 people to develop small lists of priorities. What techniques would you employ to accomplish this work?

11. Intellectual capital and knowledge assets are parts of knowledge management. Consider that, at your facility, supervisors and managers are creating case studies that reflect positive communications to encourage employees to have a stronger connection with the organization's mission. Discuss the components of a knowledge management system related to this situation.

12. You are managing a meeting of community leaders. The goal of the meeting is to consider ways to disseminate information about the importance of maintaining a personal health record. Many cultures are represented at the meeting, and there is a discussion about how to meet the language needs of the 24 different languages spoken in the community. An argument ensues about why only English and Spanish communication will be used in the dissemination of the information. What would you do?

## Web Assignment

1. Go to the Web (http://www.ahima.org might be a good first stop) to find articles related to natural, technical, and human threats. Write a summary of the articles you find, adding your opinion about them. Use Table 11–3 for ideas.

## The StudyWARE™ Challenge

Using the StudyWARE on your student software CD-ROM, complete the following activities:

1. Study the flash cards for Chapter 11 to review the key terms in this chapter.

2. Solve the hangman activities for Chapter 11.

3. Complete the quiz in test mode for Chapter 11. Record your score in the space below, and print out your results for your instructor.

---

**StudyWARE Quiz Chapter 11**

Date Taken: _____

Score: _____

---

## The DVD Hookup

Program 5: Organization and Management

Case 5.1: Failure to Launch

One of the coders visits the HIM director to complain that he hasn't been trained properly on the HIM department's new software. The objective of this scenario is to demonstrate the need for proper change management and training before systems are implemented.

## Case Discussion

1. What problems could have occurred in this case? What departments could have been affected?

_____

_____

_____

_____

_____

_____

2. What should the HIM director do to address this situation?

_____

_____

_____

_____

_____

_____

_____

3. How can system changes, including encoder software changes, be handled by management to ensure a smooth transition?

_____

_____

_____

4. How would you feel if you were in the coders' shoes?

_____

_____

Program 5: Organization and Management

Case 5.2: Suspending Physician Admitting Privileges

A physician loses his cool when his admissions privileges are suspended, and he confronts a HIM analyst. This is a typical HIM situation, and it takes strong conflict resolution skills on the part of the HIM staff.

## Case Discussion

1. What strategies could the HIM director use to defuse the situation?

_____

_____

_____

_____

2. What would have been a more diplomatic approach to the situation? How would you handle the physician's complaints?

_____

_____

_____

_____

3. After the confrontation is over, what should the director do?

_____

_____

_____

_____

_____

_____

_____

# CHAPTER 12

# Human Resource Management

## Learning Objectives

1. Define the concept of employment and differentiate between the various types of employees.

2. Understand the elements of the staffing process.

3. Explain the concept of the at-will employment doctrine.

4. Trace the development of employee rights.

5. List and describe the various civil rights and workplace protection laws that relate to human resource management.

6. Compare and contrast the supervisory functions involved with performance evaluations, prevention of problem behaviors, discipline and grievance, teambuilding, developing others, and telecommuting.

7. Describe the perspectives of the business community toward the concept of workforce diversity.

## Acronym Review

Write out the following acronyms.

1. FCRA: _____

2. ADEA: _____

3. ADA: _____

4. ERISA: _____

5. FMLA: _____

6. OSHA: _____

7. WARN: _____

8. USERRA: _____

9. OWBPA: _____

10. EEOC: _____

11. FLSA: _____

12. EPA: _____

## Key Terms Review

Match the terms in Column I to their definitions in Column II.

|  | Column I |  | Column II |
|---|---|---|---|
| 1. _____ | Employment | A. | Persons, businesses, or organizations that provide work, engage the services or labor, and pay for the work performed. |
| 2. _____ | Employers | B. | One who has a continuing relationship with the employer. |
| 3. _____ | Regular employee | C. | Individual who agrees to perform certain work according to her own means, manner, and methods of performance. |
| 4. _____ | Leased employees | D. | One who has been designated by specific laws as subject to the tax withholding requirements. |
| 5. _____ | Independent contractor | E. | Involves the process of providing work, engaging services or labor, and paying for work performed. |
| 6. _____ | Statutory employee | F. | Ones who are employed by a service firm and are assigned to work at a business or an organization. |

## Key Terms Review: ADA Terms to Know

Match the terms in Column I to their definitions in Column II.

|  | Column I |  | Column II |
|---|---|---|---|
| 1. _____ | Disability | A. | Physical or mental limitation of a major life activity caused by a disability. |
| 2. _____ | Reasonable accommodation | B. | A specific accommodation that creates significant difficulty or expense for the employer. |
| 3. _____ | Functional limitation | C. | Any change in the work environment or in the manner in which things are customarily done that enables a qualified person with a disability to have equal employment opportunities. |
| 4. _____ | Workplace barrier | D. | Physical or mental impairment that substantially limits one or more of the major life activities of an employee; a record of such impairment; or being regarded as having such an impairment. |
| 5. _____ | Undue hardship | E. | Any workplace obstacle, whether physical or procedural, that prevents an employee from performing the duties of the job, whether those duties are considered essential or marginal. |

## True or False

Indicate whether the following statements are true (T) or false (F). If a statement is false, rewrite it to make it true.

1. _____ Human resource management involves the strategic use of human beings within an organization to enhance an organization's efficiency and effectiveness.

_____

2. _____ The federal laws alone govern employee issues.

_____

3. _____ In general, full-time employees must work 30 hours per week or more.

_____

4. _____ Leased employees receive their paycheck and benefits from the businesses to which they are leased.

_____

5. _____ Staffing is the process of assigning workers to all positions in an organization.

_____

6. _____ Managers of employees are frequently involved in some or all aspects of staffing.

_____

7. _____ Recruitment is the process of finding employees for an organization.

_____

8. _____ Selection is the process of finding employees.

_____

9. _____ The goal of a personal interview is to assess a candidate's basic qualifications and screen out those candidates who are not qualified.

_____

10. _____ Interviews are important in the recruitment process because they allow the employer to assess the candidate.

_____

11. _____ Background checks are most useful in including candidates for consideration for positions.

_____

12. _____ If a background check results in denial of employment, the FCRA requires employers to inform the individual.

_____

13. _____ Medical exams or drug tests are usually done toward the end of the process because of the cost the employer must bear.

_____

14. _____ Selection tests are not helpful devices in the selection process because they are often geared toward the highest level of performance, even for entry-level jobs.

_____

15. _____ Pre-established selection criteria are a useful tool in the selection process.

_____

16. _____ An I-9 form is also known as the federal Employment Eligibility Verification form.

_____

17. _____ The partnership approach to training includes the supervisor and employee.

_____

18. _____ Retention efforts foster personal loyalty, professionalism, high morale, and organizational pride.

_____

19. _____ When employees increase their knowledge, skills, and abilities, they strengthen the organization as a whole.

_____

20. _____ Most employees do not view compensation as a key factor in employee retention.

_____

21. _____ Programs that recognize the balance between home and work life positively impact retention.

_____

22. _____ At-will employment is an employment arrangement that allows the employer to terminate the employee at any time and allows the employee to leave the employer at any time.

_____

23. _____ Prohibitions against sex discrimination are meant to promote work practices that are based on gender stereotypes.

_____

24. _____ Quid pro quo means expecting a person to do "this for that."

_____

25. _____ Claims of sexual harassment may be based on either the quid pro quo or hostile work environment, or both.

_____

26. _____ One form of sexual discrimination involves childbirth leave or pregnancy-related conditions.

_____

27. _____ The FMLA applies only to women because it encompasses pregnancy and childbirth.

_____

28. _____ During the hiring process, the burden rests on an individual to show that his impairment is a disability.

_____

29. _____ In HIM departments, hazardous work conditions may be ergonomic in nature.

_____

30. _____ Carpal tunnel syndrome or tendonitis are usually the fault of the employee and would not be considered a result of hazardous work conditions.

_____

31. _____ The FLSA establishes the minimum number of hours that an employee may work in a given time frame.

_____

32. _____ Many positions that are classified as executive, administrative, or professional are considered exempt under the FLSA.

_____

33. _____ FLSA applies only to in-office work and not to telecommuting.

_____

34. _____ ERISA addresses employee pensions and other benefit programs.

_____

35. _____ ERISA requires employers to establish pension and welfare plans.

_____

36. _____ Workers' compensation is designed to replace income and provide medical expenses to employees who are injured as a result of their jobs.

_____

37. _____ Workers' compensation does not offer protection to employers from being sued for those injuries that occur on the job.

_____

38. _____ Unemployment insurance provides regular income to those who have lost their jobs.

_____

39. _____ Your employer suspects that someone in the department is selling illegal drugs; therefore, they have the right to monitor phone calls.

_____

40. _____ The key to supervision is in understanding that work is done by other people rather than performing all of the work oneself.

_____

41. _____ A performance evaluation is an informal opportunity to review and evaluate an employee on a periodic basis.

_____

42. _____ A 360-degree evaluation instrument is used when all levels of an organization evaluate an employee.

_____

## Multiple Choice

Select the best response.

1. Human resource management activities cover a broad range, including:

    A) Ensuring effective recruitment

    B) Engaging in corrective/disciplinary action

    C) Handling an employee's separation from the organization

    D) All of the above

2. Employees employed by a service firm to work at a business are called:

    A) Independent contractors

    B) Statutory employees

    C) Leased employees

    D) Regular employees

3. A statutory employee:

    A) Does not fall into the category of employee

    B) Is subject to tax withholding requirements

    C) Is not categorized as independent

    D) All of the above

4. Staffing is a management process that includes:

    A) Recruiting and selecting

    B) Training and orienting to a business

    C) Employee compensation

    D) All of the above

5. The FCRA requires an employer to inform an individual of the type of adverse information contained in a credit check report and to:

    A) Provide a copy of the credit check report

    B) Provide a description of her rights under the FCRA

    C) Give the person an opportunity to contest the information

    D) All of the above

6. Formal compensation in return for an employee's service or merit is called:

    A) Retention

    B) A recognition program

    C) A reward program

    D) Supplemental benefits

7. Formal acknowledgement programs are called:

   A) Retention

   B) Recognition programs

   C) Rewards

   D) Supplemental benefits

8. Health care providers are expected to minimize hazardous work conditions in health care by:

   A) Operating effective infection control practices

   B) Forming effective infection control committees

   C) Applying safety precautions such as those involving the handling of bodily fluids

   D) All of the above

9. Which of the following is not required by OSHA regulations?

   A) Keeping injury and illness logs

   B) Keeping safety training records

   C) Keeping medical records of employees who have been exposed to hazardous substances or harmful physical agents

   D) Keeping medical records of all employees in case of complaints of hazardous conditions

10. During an evaluation of a supervisor, a manager may look at whether the supervisor provided direction to others as well as whether others were willing to accept and support the supervisor's leadership efforts. The manager is evaluating the function of:

    A) Organizing

    B) Directing

    C) Controlling

    D) Leading

## Complete the Table: Know Your Civil Rights Laws

Complete the table by describing the following civil rights laws.

| | |
|---|---|
| Civil Rights Act of 1964 | |
| Equal Pay Act | |
| Sexual Harassment Guidelines (Title VII) | |

| | |
|---|---|
| Family and Medical Leave Act | _____ _____ |
| Age Discrimination in Employment Act | _____ _____ |
| Americans with Disabilities Act | _____ _____ |
| Worker Adjustment and Retraining Notification Act | _____ _____ |
| Employee Retirement Income Security Act | _____ _____ |

## Matching

Write the appropriate word from the following list next to its meaning. Note: words may be used more than once.

Compensation

Wages

Salary

Supplemental benefits

Call-in/overtime pay

Incentive

1. _____ Additional compensation an employee receives beyond the base salary or wage.

2. _____ Employees are paid the same amount each pay period regardless of any modest difference in total working hours.

3. _____ Wages, salaries, incentives, and supplemental benefits provided to staff.

4. _____ Does not inflate the salary structure and can be tied to profits and revenues.

5. _____ Commissions, bonuses, and stock options are examples.

6. _____ Influences employee recruitment, satisfaction, motivation, and retention.

7. _____ Include legally required benefits, such as social security.

8. _____ Employees are paid only for the hours they actually work.

9. _____ Services and programs offered to employees beyond the base salary or wage.

10. _____ Rate of pay given on a weekly, monthly, or yearly schedule.

11. _____ An hourly rate of pay and the basis used for many blue-collar workers.

12. _____ Basis used for white-collar workers.

## Short Answer

1. You are an independent contractor providing coding services for three long-term care facilities. What does the contractor-employee relationship mean?

_____

_____

2. A reference check serves two purposes. What are they?

_____

_____

3. Selection tests are administered to help employers place applicants in suitable jobs. List three examples.

_____

_____

4. Indicate whether the following activities are a function of staffing (1), recruitment (2), or selection (3):

_____ Assigning workers to positions in an organization

_____ Finding employees for an organization

_____ Process to retain employees

_____ Termination of employees when needed

_____ Internal posting of jobs

_____ Use of advertising

_____ Choosing who will work for the organization

_____ Involves a reference check

_____ Involves a background check

5. What law requires employers to operate a place of employment that is free from recognized hazards that are likely to cause serious injury or a fatality? Discuss its importance on health care in particular.

_____

6. Which laws offer protections to veterans and military personnel who are called up for short-term emergency duty or extended reserve duty?

_____

7. An HIM employee slips on some paper records that are scattered on the floor. What should the employee do to protect himself in case he is injured as a result?

_____

_____

_____

8. You are a supervisor of five coders. One coder has complained about two other coders not doing enough work. You realize that you have not performed any performance evaluations for well over a year. You decide to do so for all employees. What are some steps you would take, and what would you tell the coders?

_____

_____

_____

_____

9. A health care organization had hired six male lab technicians in Year 1 and four female lab technicians in Year 5. Although all 10 lab technicians currently perform the same job, the 6 male lab technicians receive greater hourly pay rates than the 4 female lab technicians because of their seniority and number of years with the organization. What laws will be used to determine any unfair practices in this case?

_____

_____

10. Describe the process of completing a written evaluation.

_____

_____

_____

## Case Exploration

1. Some background checks for a position in health care include:

A) Examining credit history
B) Fingerprinting
C) Tax checks

Discuss your personal ideas about these types of background checks for a department director position within a health care agency. Discuss the pros and cons.

2. You are the person responsible for conducting a basic orientation for the medical students at your facility. Develop a PowerPoint presentation of key areas to cover.

3. You supervise the coders at a hospital and you are having a hard time retaining them due to the distances they drive, dense traffic problems, and (as a result) more time away from their families. What retention strategies could you consider?

_____

4. The manager you work for has made it clear that any employee asked to do jury duty is to try to get out of it. You have an employee who takes jury duty very seriously and you have been told by the CEO to warn the employee of the possibility of being fired. What laws do you reference and what do you tell the CEO?

_____

_____

_____

5. While in the lunchroom of the hospital in which you work, you hear a supervisor tell racial and religious jokes. She brags about firing an atheist, claiming that she does not need the employee destroying the open religious environment. What law(s) are being violated? What would you do?

_____

_____

6. An employee comes to you and tells you that she is having difficulty performing her job due to chronic fatigue syndrome. As her supervisor, role-play the process you need to go through to determine if/how you can accommodate this employee.

7. Jennifer, the supervisor of coding, is being evaluated by Jackson, the department manager. Role-play the process of evaluating Jennifer's performance with regard to planning, organizing, directing, controlling, and leading.

## The StudyWARE™ Challenge

Using the StudyWARE on your student software CD-ROM, complete the following activities:

1. Study the flash cards for Chapter 12 to review the key terms in this chapter.

2. Solve the crossword puzzle for Chapter 12.

3. Complete the quiz in test mode for Chapter 12. Record your score in the space below, and print out your results for your instructor.

> **StudyWARE Quiz Chapter 12**
>
> Date Taken: _____
>
> Score: _____

## The DVD Hookup

Program 5: Organization and Management

Case 5.3: Employee Counseling

The HIM director asks the HIM coordinator to come to her office to discuss the coordinator's three-month evaluation. In this scenario, the new HIM coordinator has made a number of errors.

## Case Discussion

1. Was the new employee evaluation handled appropriately and in a timely manner? How soon should the HIM director follow up with her?

_____

_____

_____

_____

2. What could the HIM director have done differently during Amanda's probationary period that would have contributed to a better overall job performance?

_____

_____

_____

3. What might the director recommend to improve HIPAA compliance in Amanda's job performance? What training does Amanda need?

_____

_____

_____

_____

4. Why should there be a probationary evaluation?

_____

_____

_____

_____

Program 5: Organization and Management

Case 5.4: Impromptu Interview

An HIM clerk interviews with the HIM director for an entry-level coding position. The HIM director agrees to work with the employee to groom her for the position. Although not all hospitals are willing to spend a lot of time training coders, many will do so, especially when they desperately need their services.

## Case Discussion

1. How should Mary have prepared for the interview?

_____

2. What can Mary do to make the next interview more positive?

_____

_____

_____

_____

3. What can the HIM director do to help Mary prepare to move into coding?

_____

_____

4. What problems might the HIM director cause by allowing Mary to spend time coding?

_____

_____

_____

_____

5. Why would the facility want to give coding tests to potential coders?

_____

_____

# CHAPTER 13

# Information Systems and Technology

## Learning Objectives

1. Compare and contrast the computer concepts of hardware and software.

2. Recognize the basic units of a personal computer and a computer room.

3. Differentiate between the software concepts of operating systems, application programs, utility programs, and programming languages.

4. Define the term *information systems life cycle* and explain its application in project management.

5. Understand communication technologies such as networks, the Internet, and security measures.

6. Define the term *informatics* and describe its application in the health care field.

7. Distinguish between the terms *electronic health, e-health organizations,* and *e-health consumers.*

8. Describe the technology applications of telemedicine, voice recognition, and digital imaging.

9. Understand the functionalities of an electronic health record.

## Acronyms Review

Write out the following acronyms.

1. LAN: _____

2. MAN: _____

3. WAN: _____

4. VPN: _____

5. HTML: _____

6. XML: _____

7. SGML: _____

8. PDA: _____

9. IP: _____

10. WWW: _____

11. ISP: _____

12. ASPs: _____

## Key Terms Review

Match the terms in Column I to their definitions in Column II.

| | Column I | | Column II |
|---|---|---|---|
| 1. \_\_\_\_\_ | Monitor | A. | All the physical electronic components of a computer system—those things that one can touch. |
| 2. \_\_\_\_\_ | Mouse | B. | Reproduce on paper the text and image found on the computer. |
| 3. \_\_\_\_\_ | Keyboard | C. | Device that depends on reading and writing data from a rotating disk for its operation. |
| 4. \_\_\_\_\_ | Disk drive | D. | Optical storage medium. |
| 5. \_\_\_\_\_ | Hard drive | E. | Displays the output of a computer. |
| 6. \_\_\_\_\_ | Floppy disk | F. | Computer that contains a central processing unit. |
| 7. \_\_\_\_\_ | CD-ROM drive | G. | Convert printed pages or graphic images into a file, which can be stored in a computer and retrieved by an end user. |
| 8. \_\_\_\_\_ | Flash drive | H. | Programs that tell the computer what to do and how to do it. |
| 9. \_\_\_\_\_ | Hardware | I. | Sometimes called processors, these are the most important piece of hardware for personal computers. |
| 10. \_\_\_\_\_ | Software | J. | Sometimes referred to as a jump drive; a small, lightweight removable data storage device. |
| 11. \_\_\_\_\_ | Personal computer | K. | Small hand control with buttons that control the position of the cursor on the monitor screen. |
| 12. \_\_\_\_\_ | Central processing units | L. | Device used to input numbers, characters, and commands into a computer. |
| 13. \_\_\_\_\_ | Printers | M. | Removable flexible disk made of plastic coasted with a magnetic oxide layer. |
| 14. \_\_\_\_\_ | Scanners | N. | Magnetic storage device that stores individual data on the surface of a rapidly rotating metal disk that is coated with a film of magnetizable material. |

## True or False

Indicate whether the following statements are true (T) or false (F). If a statement is false, rewrite it to make it true.

1. _____ Voice recognition technology is also referred to as interactive voice recognition.

_____

2. _____ The need for and cost of storage space is greater when using an EHR.

_____

3. _____ Different accrediting and licensing requirements dealing with the content of a medical record apply to an EHR than to a traditional health record.

_____

4. _____ Telemedicine is sometimes referred to as telehealth.

_____

5. _____ Hardware is the term for the programs that tell the computer what to do and how to do it.

_____

6. _____ Information systems life cycle refers to the succession of stages of an information system.

_____

7. _____ Besides computers, networks can include printers, fax modems, scanners, and CD-ROM drives.

_____

## Multiple Choice

Select the best response.

1. Electronic health (e-health) includes:

   A) E-health organizations

   B) E-health consumers

   C) Consumers and business

   D) All of the above

2. Telemedicine:

   A) Connects the patient to the health care provider through the use of information technologies

   B) Is used only in remote areas

   C) Cannot legally be used to diagnose

   D) Has mandated coverage by Medicare in all cases

3. In an electronic health record system, which of the following is a system of scanning and storing?

   A) VRT

   B) Digital imaging

   C) MRI

   D) Interactive voice recognition

4. The clinician is in a better position to recognize and treat medical problems and to avoid redundant testing if he applies the following functionality of EHRs:

   A) Order entry and management

   B) Results management

   C) Administrative processes

   D) Patient support

5. Among the most significant benefits of this is the reduction in the incidence of medication errors:

   A) Administrative processes

   B) Results management

   C) Order entry and management

   D) Clinical decision support

6. The EHR functionality that includes items such as preventive service reminders and alerts concerning possible drug interactions is:

   A) Order entry and management

   B) Health information and data

   C) Results management

   D) Clinical decision support

## Matching

Match the terms in Column I to their definitions in Column II.

| | Column I | | Column II |
|---|---|---|---|
| 1. _____ | Peripheral | A. | A form of computer hardware that is added to a host computer to expand its capabilities. |
| 2. _____ | Mainframe | B. | Performs tasks on behalf of the end user. |
| 3. _____ | Server | C. | Programming language that allows for the display of information in a similar format on different operating systems and system hardware. |
| 4. _____ | Mobile | D. | An object that can be carried or wheeled from place to place. |
| 5. _____ | Laptop computer | E. | An object equipped with a special card that enables it to broadcast and receive radio or cellular signals that reach a network via access points. |
| 6. _____ | Personal digital assistant | F. | Technical specifications or other precise criteria to be used consistently as rules, guidelines, or other definitions of characteristics. |
| 7. _____ | Wireless | G. | XML is based on this separate language. |
| 8. _____ | Operating system | H. | Computer containing a powerful central processing unit that controls the activity of the dummy monitor. |
| 9. _____ | Application program | I. | Computer that can be conveniently held in a person's hand. |
| 10. _____ | Utility program | J. | Works with raw data. |
| 11. _____ | Programming language | K. | Computer that can be conveniently balanced on a person's knees. |
| 12. _____ | Hypertext markup language | L. | Software that controls how the computer works. |
| 13. _____ | Extensible markup language | M. | Performs simple operations on files created by other programs. |

14. _____ Standard generalized    N.  Created language used to write application and utility programs.
markup language

15. _____ Standards    O.  Computers that provide shared services to other computers on a network.

## Matching

Match the terms in Column I to their definitions in Column II.

|  | **Column I** |  | **Column II** |
|---|---|---|---|
| 1. _____ | Versions | A. | Persons who gain unauthorized access to computer systems and networks. |
| 2. _____ | Network | B. | Criminal hackers. |
| 3. _____ | Internet | C. | Means to regulate access to and ensure preservation of data. |
| 4. _____ | Modem | D. | Name given to a server or group of servers connected to the Internet. |
| 5. _____ | ISDN | E. | Upgrades to software applications that provide new functionality. |
| 6. _____ | Cable modems | F. | Work via cable telephone connections. |
| 7. _____ | DSL | G. | Blueprints used to resume immediate computer operations in the event of a problem. |
| 8. _____ | IP address | H. | Copying on a regular basis the data stored on a computer or server so that it can be restored should the original data be destroyed. |
| 9. _____ | Domain name | I. | Device that allows a computer to transfer information over a telephone line. |
| 10. _____ | Portal | J. | Internet Protocol addresses that are activated to provide a connection between a browser and another site on the Internet. |
| 11. _____ | Links | K. | Intranet system that allows selected external users limited access to the private networks. |
| 12. _____ | Intranet | L. | Public digital data network intended to supplant traditional telephone system. |
| 13. _____ | Extranet | M. | Process of ensuring that people are who they say they are when using a computer. |
| 14. _____ | Security | N. | Unique number that is assigned to each host computer connected to the Internet. |
| 15. _____ | Authentication | O. | Level of access granted by the operating system to a person or group of persons. |
| 16. _____ | Permission | P. | Collection of computers connected together by way of cables or wireless links so that they can exchange data with one another. |
| 17. _____ | Encryption | Q. | Transmits all data as digital signals but does not require access to television connections. |

| | | | |
|---|---|---|---|
| 18. _____ | Firewall | R. | Web site that offers free entry to numerous other sites through the use of links. |
| 19. _____ | Virus scan | S. | Worldwide network of small networks. |
| 20. _____ | Computer virus | T. | Special hardware or software placed between a computer and the Internet that serves to monitor all traffic passing between them. |
| 21. _____ | Hackers | U. | Process of searching a hard drive or network data stream to detect the presence of computer viruses. |
| 22. _____ | Crackers | V. | Small computer program capable of copying itself from one computer to another. |
| 23. _____ | Disaster recovery plans | W. | Operates as a private network that is accessible only within one organization. |
| 24. _____ | Backup regime | X. | Mechanism employed so that no third party can eavesdrop on communication. |

## Complete the Table

Describe the components of the following subsets of the health care informatics disciplines. On the right side of the chart, list the descriptions of the informatics systems listed in the left-hand column.

| | |
|---|---|
| Medical Informatics | |
| Health Care Informatics | |
| Clinical Informatics | |
| Dental Informatics | |
| Public Health Informatics | |
| Nursing Informatics | |
| Consumer Health Informatics | |
| Educational Informatics | |

## Short Answer

1. What is the difference between a LAN, WAN, MAN, and VPN?

_____

_____

_____

_____

2. Describe the importance of public health informatics in today's health care global environment.

_____

_____

_____

3. What is the relationship between CPOE and e-prescribing?

_____

_____

_____

_____

4. What is the difference between an EHR and a clinical information system?

_____

5. What are eight functionalities that are common to an EHR as defined by the Institute of Medicine?

_____

_____

6. Explain the differences between authorship and authentication.

_____

_____

## Case Exploration

1. You leave your job at a large ambulatory clinic and pass the trash containers for the facility. The trash containers have locks on them to provide security for PHI. You notice that someone has laid a bag of office trash on top of the locked bin. You can easily see through the trash bag and notice one page that has a red stamp that says "CONFIDENTIAL" on it and another that is a report of HIV/AIDS patients treated at the clinic. However, you are late picking up your child from day care. What is the security issue in this situation? What is your ethical obligation? How will you handle this situation given all of the factors listed above?

2. You are asked to sit on a committee to develop part of the electronic health record at a long-term care facility. Members of the team include a nursing administrator, the chief information officer, an information technology specialist, and yourself, the director of HIM. Judging from your past experiences with IT, there seems to be a problem with miscommunication. What would you do to improve the communication with IT?

## Web Assignment

1. Go to http://www.ahima.org, http://www.himss.org, or another Web site of your choosing, and find one article on the issue of human social engineering and health care.

## The StudyWARE™ Challenge

Using the StudyWARE on your student software CD-ROM, complete the following activities:

1. Study the flash cards for Chapter 13 to review the key terms in this chapter.

2. Solve the hangman activities for Chapter 13.

3. Complete the quiz in test mode for Chapter 13. Record your score in the space below, and print out your results for your instructor.

> **StudyWARE Quiz Chapter 13**
>
> Date Taken: _____
>
> Score: _____

## The DVD Hookup

Program 4: Information Technology and Systems

Case 4.1: Selecting a Master Patient Index

The chief information officer tries to help the HIM director with her task of choosing a master patient index (MPI) system. Choosing an information system is not something to be taken lightly. It requires planning, knowing what you need, and locating the system that meets your needs. This case utilizes the MPI to illustrate the problem, but the system involved could vary.

## Case Discussion

1. Can you identify problems with the way the decision is being handled?

_____

_____

_____

_____

2.  What strategies could have been employed to prevent decisions being made based on opinions?

_____

_____

_____

_____

3.  What evaluation criteria could have been used?

_____

Program 4: Information Technology and Systems

Case 4.3: Breach of Information Security

The hospital administrator receives a strange call from the editor of a local paper regarding some of the hospital's patient records. Facilities are required to terminate an employee's access to the information system when he or she leaves the covered entity's employ. In this scenario, the facility failed to do so, and the end result was that a former employee released protected health information to a newspaper.

## Case Discussion

1.  Identify how this situation could have happened. What could have been done to prevent these breaches of security?

_____

_____

_____

_____

2.  What types of information will the HIM director be looking for in the audit log?

_____

_____

3.  What mitigation would you recommend?

_____

_____

_____

# CHAPTER 14

# Financial Management

## Learning Objectives

1. Understand the three parts of the finance cycle.

2. Identify the uses and users of accounting information.

3. Compare and contrast a balance sheet, income statement, and cash flow statement.

4. Differentiate between managerial accounting and financial accounting.

5. Define a budget and describe the ways in which organizations rely upon budgets.

6. Trace the stages in the procurement process.

7. Identify the contents of a request for proposal.

## Acronym Review

Write out the following acronyms.

1. CFO: _____

2. GAAP: _____

3. RFI: _____

4. RFP: _____

5. RFQ: _____

6. FASB: _____

## Key Terms Review

Match the terms in Column I to their definitions in Column II.

| | Column I | | Column II |
|---|---|---|---|
| 1. _____ | Assets | A. | The amount of money an organization owes. |
| 2. _____ | Liabilities | B. | When you deposit money with the bank. |
| 3. _____ | Owner's equity | C. | The amount invested in the start-up of a health care organization by the owner. |
| 4. _____ | Credits | D. | The organization's real property. |
| 5. _____ | Debits | E. | When you remove money from the bank. |

| | | | |
|---|---|---|---|
| 6. _____ | Journal | F. | Separate recording made for each asset and liability. |
| 7. _____ | Account | G. | Book or document in which each transaction is entered in chronological order. |
| 8. _____ | General ledger | H. | Cash received. |
| 9. _____ | Receipt | I. | Complete set of accounts established and maintained by the organization. |

## True or False

Indicate whether the following statements are true (T) or false (F). If a statement is false, rewrite it to make it true.

1. _____ Government regulators examine financial statements on a routine basis to determine a business's financial condition.

_____

2. _____ It is the role of accountants to assess the organization's financial performance.

_____

3. _____ Capital budget officers oversee planning for large tangible projects.

_____

4. _____ Department managers oversee planning for large tangible projects.

_____

5. _____ For those responsible for the coding function, reimbursement to the organization is affected by the accuracy and timeliness with which coding is performed.

_____

6. _____ If coding occurs less accurately and takes more time, reimbursement is minimized.

_____

7. _____ It is important for all members of a health care organization, from the line staff to the supervisors to the senior executives, to share an understanding of financial management.

_____

8. _____ Only managers and senior executives need to be concerned about the financial management of a health care agency.

_____

9. _____ Finance is the science of money, credit, and banking.

_____

10. _____ Accounting is a forward-looking activity.

_____

11. _____ Budgeting is a forward-looking activity.

_____

12. _____ Financial accounting refers to the day-to-day management of an organization's cash, credit, inventory, liabilities, and expenses.

_____

13. _____ Bookkeeping is the record-keeping aspect of accounting.

_____

14. _____ Internal controls in accounting procedures minimize errors and fraud.

_____

15. _____ Audits serve to discover mistakes in accounting procedures after their occurrence.

_____

16. _____ The work done by internal auditors is often considered objective and unbiased, which provides confidence to investors, lenders, and regulatory authorities.

_____

17. _____ An external auditor begins with the source document and follows it through the steps in the bookkeeping process.

_____

18. _____ An unqualified audit report is of the highest level of audit reports.

_____

19. _____ A qualified audit report indicates that the auditors are satisfied with the organization's financial health and practices or its legal compliance.

_____

20. _____ An income statement summarizes revenue and expenses at a specified point of time.

_____

21. _____ A cash flow statement notes profits and extraordinary gains and losses.

_____

22. _____ Organizations that experience broad fluctuations between the receipt and payment of cash would be more likely to use accrual accounting.

_____

23. _____ A budget is an organization's revenue and expenditure plan.

_____

24. _____ Financial reports are used by groups outside the organization to assess the financial performance and viability of the organization.

_____

25. _____ Financial accounting focuses on the big picture of the organization.

_____

26. _____ Managerial accounting focuses on the big picture of an organization.

_____

27. _____ A budget is a part of management control.

_____

28. _____ Variances are inconsistencies between numbers or statements.

_____

29. _____ Procurement is a part of financial management.

_____

30. _____ The procurement function poses the potential to damage the organization's chances for financial success.

_____

31. _____ The identification of the need to purchase goods or contract for services requires specifications.

_____

32. _____ In the procurement process, the "buyer" is responsible for communicating with the vendor.

_____

33. _____ RFPs are done before RFIs.

_____

34. _____ An RFI is a formal document seeking information about products or services available in the marketplace that can meet the organization's needs.

_____

## Multiple Choice

Select the best response.

1. The supervisor of five employees in coding needs to develop a plan to increase the salary of her staff. The first person to contact about this is the:

   A) Human resource director

   B) Facilities accountant who accesses the organization's finances

   C) Director of the department who manages the budget

   D) Facilities controller who has the best knowledge of payroll

2. The position best suited to assess an organization's financial performance is:

    A) Department manager

    B) Capital budget officer

    C) Accountant

    D) First-line supervisor

3. Finance can be thought of as a cycle that primarily focuses on:

    A) Assessing the financial performance and health of an organization

    B) Applying that information to create a plan for future performance

    C) Executing that plan

    D) All of the above

4. The person who oversees the organization's assets and financial planning is the:

    A) CEO

    B) CFO

    C) CMIO

    D) CIO

5. Budgeting is linked to:

    A) The planning function of management

    B) Future organizational strategy

    C) Short-term goals of the organization

    D) All of the above

6. Accounting is:

    A) A system used to record, state, or audit business transactions

    B) A distinct discipline that has its own standards, practices, and language

    C) Known as the "language" of finance because it is used to record financial transactions

    D) All of the above

7. Establishing limits upon the authority of individuals to act within an organization is:

    A) Delegation of authority

    B) Separation of duties

    C) Safeguarding of assets

    D) All of the above

8. Which of the following is a serious matter in an audit report?

   A) A finding

   B) A material strength

   C) An unqualified audit

   D) All of the above

9. GAAP are issued by the:

   A) CEO

   B) CFO

   C) FASB

   D) FAA

10. Long-term budgets:

    A) Are less definite

    B) Are more definite

    C) Are more detailed

    D) All of the above

11. A budget that focuses on administrative costs, research and development costs, and marketing costs is:

    A) An expense budget

    B) A cash budget

    C) A capital expenditure

    D) A sales budget

12. This type of budget focuses on the volume and type of health care services provided in the past and compares it to an estimate of future needs.

    A) Expense

    B) Sales

    C) Statistics

    D) Master

13. Financial accounting refers to the periodic assessment of an organization's financial health on this basis.

    A) Weekly, monthly, annual

    B) Monthly, quarterly, annual

    C) Annual, 5-, and 10-year projection

    D) Quarterly, semiannual, and annual

14. A financial report that summarizes the true financial condition of an organization, showing its assets, liabilities, and the owner's equity, is a(n):

    A) Balance sheet

    B) Cash flow statement

    C) Income statement

    D) Audit report

15. The request for proposal includes:

    A) An introduction to the organization

    B) General contractual specifications

    C) Evaluation criteria

    D) All of the above

16. Budgets are linked to:

    A) Planning

    B) Variances

    C) Forecasting

    D) All of the above

17. Procurement activities include:

    A) Identification of vendors

    B) Solicitation of bids

    C) Monitoring contracts

    D) All of the above

18. The separation of duties involved in the purchasing of goods necessitates:

    A) The use of one person to authorize the purchase

    B) A second person to receive the goods

    C) A third person to keep records and arrange payment

    D) All of the above

19. Specifications are features required of a product or service and may take the form of:

    A) Quality and quantity

    B) Price and service

    C) Performance

    D) All of the above

20. Purchase orders:

    A) Are legally binding

    B) Are not legally binding

    C) Can usually be signed by any employee

    D) Are needed only for large-bid items

21. An invitation to bid for a contract is done via:

    A) RFI

    B) RFP

    C) RCA

    D) RFQ

## Select All That Apply

1. Financial reports of a health care organization are generally reviewed by (select all that apply):

_____  Government regulators

_____  CFO

_____  CEO

_____  Coders

_____  Transcription contractor

_____  Investors of the agency

_____  Accrediting agencies

## Short Answer

1. You are on the health care facilities finance committee at a very small clinic. The clinic recently changed from a manual to an electronic financial system. Discuss some possibilities for enhancing safeguarding assets within the system.

_____

_____

2. Which financial person within the organization should be approached to discuss the implementation of EHRs in the next two years?

_____

_____

3. What is the relationship between the speed and quality of information shared with members of the health care team?

_____

4. What are the benefits of using both internal and external auditors?

_____

_____

_____

5. The medical reimbursement specialist records the income (revenue) to be received from the patient during Month 1. The medical reimbursement specialist also records the same rent, supplies, utilities, and salaries that were paid out during Month 1. What accounting method is used? What will it tell the clinic?

_____

6. A physician provides services to a patient in her office in Month 1 but receives payment for those services in Month 3. However, the physician records disbursements for rent, supplies, utilities, and salaries during Month 1 because those were necessary to conduct business at the time the patient was seen in the office. In this scenario, does the physician lose money during Month 1 ?

_____

7. The RFP has been released to potential vendors. One vendor poses a question to the organization. Does the answer to the question need to be shared with all vendors? Why or why not?

_____

_____

8. Discuss the components of the bidding process.

_____

_____

_____

_____

9. Sometimes a dispute of contract occurs. What steps are taken to resolve the dispute?

_____

_____

_____

_____

10. Your organization is involved in procuring several new computers. What are the steps involved in doing this?

_____

_____

## Case Exploration

1. As a director of the HIM department with a master's degree in business administration at a small ambulatory medical clinic, you are asked to take on the additional role of controller. Role-play this situation and describe your responsibilities in the financial cycle.

2. As a long-term department manager in the surgical center, you are asked to explain the basic terms of financial accounting to three other (newer) department managers. Develop a PowerPoint presentation to do so.

3. Your organization is developing an electronic record system, and you are on a development team that will write an RFP. Discuss where and how your input as an HIM is important.

## The StudyWARE™ Challenge

Using the StudyWARE on your student software CD-ROM, complete the following activities:

1. Study the flash cards for Chapter 14 to review the key terms in this chapter.

2. Solve the crossword puzzle for Chapter 14.

3. Complete the quiz in test mode for Chapter 14. Record your score in the space below, and print out your results for your instructor.

---

**StudyWARE Quiz Chapter 14**

Date Taken: _____

Score: _____

---

## The DVD Hookup

Program 4: Information Technology and Systems

Case 4.4: EHR without HIM

The HIM director goes to see the chief information officer when she finds out that the HIM department wasn't consulted about the purchase of an electronic health record system. The committee assumed—incorrectly—that because they were looking at a computer system, the HIM director did not need to be involved. It did not take long for the HIM director to list off the many issues that the committee failed to address in the request for proposal.

## Case Discussion

1. Why would, or should, HIM professionals be involved in the implementation of an EHR system?

_____

_____

_____

2. Did the HIM director act appropriately by going to the CIO and asking to be involved?

_____

_____

_____

_____

3. What types of functionality should be part of an EHR system?

_____

_____

4. Why should the EHR team be interdisciplinary?

_____

_____

_____

_____

# CHAPTER 15

# Reimbursement Methodologies

## Learning Objectives

1. Understand the concept of reimbursement methodologies as they relate to a health care organization's financial well-being.

2. Define the term *third-party payer* and identify examples in the governmental and nongovernmental sectors.

3. Describe the different forms of managed care organizations.

4. Compare and contrast the many payment methodologies used in health care.

5. Explain the processes involved in revenue cycle management.

## Acronym Review

Write out the following acronyms.

1. SNF PPS: _____

2. RUG-III: _____

3. OPPS: _____

4. APC: _____

5. HH PPS: _____

6. HHRG: _____

7. IRF PPS: _____

8. CMG: _____

9. HCPCS: _____

10. HMO: _____

11. IDS: _____

12. POS: _____

13. PPO: _____

14. DRG: _____

## Key Terms Review

Match the terms in Column I to their definitions in Column II.

|  | Column I |  | Column II |
|---|---|---|---|

1. _____ Capitation

A. The principle requiring health care providers to make reasonable efforts to limit the treatments and services rendered the patient to those that are necessary to accomplish the intended purpose of care.

2. _____ Diagnosis-related groups

B. A payment method that establishes rates, prices, or budgets for future reimbursement before the health care provider delivers services or incurs costs.

3. _____ Medical necessity

C. Independent organizations possessing expertise in all or a portion of the claims process that administer health insurance plans on behalf of companies.

4. _____ Prospective payment system

D. A setup in which physicians may only treat those patients who are members of an HMO plan.

5. _____ Resource-based relative value scale

E. A payment method wherein a fixed amount is paid to a health care provider for a group of specified health services on a periodic basis, regardless of the quantity or nature of the services rendered.

6. _____ Inflation

F. The efficient and effective use of administrative and clinical functions to capture, manage, and collect revenue related to the delivery of patient services.

7. _____ Usual, customary, and reasonable

G. A classification system that groups patients who are medically related by diagnosis, treatment, and length of stay, using ICD-9-CM codes.

8. _____ Revenue cycle management

H. A DRG-type system adopted by Medicare for reimbursement of physician services.

9. _____ Third-party administrators

I. A method used to determine health care payments, combining the provider's usual charge for a given procedure or service, the amount customarily charged for the same procedure or service by other providers in the area, and the reasonable costs of a procedure or service following medical review of the case.

10. _____ Closed-panel arrangement

J. The persistent rise in the average level of prices.

## True or False

Indicate whether the following statements are true (T) or false (F). If a statement is false, rewrite it to make it true.

1. _____ Reimbursement is focused on finance and the treatment of the patient.

_____

2. _____ Forty percent of third-party payers are represented by the federal government.

_____

3. _____ Medicaid is a joint federal-state program.

_____

4. _____ Health care providers cannot restrict the number of patients they see from the Medicaid program.

_____

5. _____ Workers' compensation is a federal and state program.

_____

6. _____ Workers' compensation only provides compensation for health care costs of those at work.

_____

7. _____ A PPO is a prepaid, organized system for providing comprehensive health care services within a geographic area to all persons under contract, emphasizing preventive medicine.

_____

8. _____ A POS is an entity composed of health care providers who contract with an employer or private health insurance company to deliver services at a discounted rate in return for a promise of a high volume of patients.

_____

9. _____ Using an EPO, the patient must stay within the provider network to receive care.

_____

10. _____ An IDS is a network of organizations that provides a full spectrum of coordinated health care services.

_____

11. _____ A closed-panel arrangement means physicians do not join in any profits that an organization generates.

_____

12. _____ Using an IPA, an organized group or association serves as the buffer between the HMO and the individual physician.

_____

13. _____ Using an EPO, the patient must stay in the network or pay the total bill for out-of-network care.

_____

14. _____ Using a POS, a patient chooses the type of provider from whom she will receive care, at or near the point of time when she will receive the care.

_____

15. _____ Vertical integration in an IDS offers the patient "one-stop shopping" for health care service.

_____

16. _____ A chargemaster is a listing of all the elements involved in providing the service to be billed.

_____

17. _____ Utilizing UCE, the health care provider is reimbursed for the costs incurred.

_____

18. _____ A certificate-of-need program requires health care facilities to justify to a state agency the need to purchase new equipment.

_____

19. _____ A PPS is a retrospective reimbursement system.

_____

20. _____ A PPS is a payment method in which reimbursement is based on services used.

_____

## Multiple Choice

Select the best response.

1. Marine Sergeant Catherine Monarez died in the line of duty. Her sons will be covered by:

    A) Medicare

    B) TRICARE

    C) CHAMPUS

    D) CHAMPVA

2. The program designed to provide health services to native American Indians and native Alaskans is:

    A) CHAMPUS

    B) IHS

    C) IDS

    D) CHAMPVA

3. By 1998, some states saw _____ of their population enrolled in managed care plans.

    A) 25 percent

    B) 35 percent

    C) 45 percent

    D) 55 percent

4. The gatekeeper in a managed care plan is:

    A) The person who makes appointments

    B) The triage nurse

    C) The primary care provider

    D) The care line provider

5. The staff model in an HMO:

   A) Considers physicians employees

   B) Does not affect physicians' independence as contractors

   C) Promotes an open model arrangement

   D) All of the above

6. A physician is not part of a closed-panel management in an:

   A) HMO network model

   B) HMO IPA model

   C) HMO mixed model

   D) HMO staff model

7. A health system that concentrates on delivering a single type of service (e.g., acute care hospitals) to a geographic region is considered:

   A) Vertical

   B) Horizontal

   C) Matrix

   D) Open-paneled

8. A payment methodology that uses a retrospective payment system is:

   A) Fee for service

   B) Prospective payment

   C) Resource-based relative value

   D) Capitation

9. A payment methodology that includes a case mix analysis is:

   A) Fee for service

   B) Prospective payment system

   C) Resource-based relative value

   D) Capitation

10. Which payment methodology poses a higher economic risk to the payer?

    A) Fee for service

    B) Prospective payment system

    C) Resource-based relative value

    D) Capitation

11. Using FFS, a patient is charged:

    A) For a distinct unit of service delivered

    B) For an identifiable unit of service delivered

    C) On a per-procedure or per-service-provided basis

    D) All of the above

12. Usual, customary, and reasonable costs are generally based on:

    A) The health care provider's usual charge for a given procedure or service

    B) The amount customarily charged for the same procedure or service by other health care providers in the area

    C) The reasonable costs of procedures or services for a given patient following medical review of the case

    D) All of the above

13. Using a PPS, the health care provider:

    A) Receives a predetermined rate based on a patient's treatment

    B) Receives total coverage for the services the provider gives

    C) Receives any surplus from payment of service

    D) A and C

## Matching

The following terms are essential to your understanding of insurance. Match the terms in Column I to their definitions in Column II.

| | Column I | | Column II |
|---|---|---|---|
| 1. _____ | Private health care insurance | A. | Health care services that have previously been identified as reimbursable under the insurance plan. |
| 2. _____ | Insured | B. | The one holding the policy/receiving the care. |
| 3. _____ | Premium | C. | A specific amount or fee prepaid to an insurer on a regular basis. |
| 4. _____ | Insurer | D. | A means of financing health care in which the insured prepays a specific amount to an insurer on a regular basis in exchange for the insurer's agreement to pay the health care provider's charges for the treatment rendered to the insured, up to previously specified limits. |
| 5. _____ | Blue Cross/Blue Shield Association | E. | Principle requiring health care providers to make reasonable efforts to limit the treatments and services rendered the patient to those that are necessary to accomplish the intended purpose of care. |
| 6. _____ | Coverage | F. | The insurance company that agrees to pay the health care provider's charges for the treatment rendered to the insured, up to previously specified limits. |

7. _____ Medical necessity

    G. The single largest trade association of private health care insurers in the United States.

8. _____ Third-party administrators

    H. Health plans that integrate fully the financial and delivery aspects of health care.

9. _____ Managed care

    I. Independent organizations that administer self-insurance plans as a means to minimize overhead costs.

## Short Answer

1. List the four eligibility requirements for Medicare.

_____

_____

_____

_____

2. List the eligibility requirements for Medicaid.

_____

_____

_____

_____

_____

3. Describe how balance billing is determined.

_____

4. Explain what "unbundling" means.

_____

_____

_____

5. The following years are important dates related to health care insurance. What happened in the following years?

1973: _____

1982: _____

_____

1985: _____

_____

1988: _____

1994: _____

_____

## Case Exploration

1.  You are the supervisor of the reimbursement area of the business office, and you are developing a basic learning module for new employees. How would you define Parts A, B, C, D of the Medicare system? Develop a learning module that will cover this material for new employees.

## The StudyWARE™ Challenge

Using the StudyWARE on your student software CD-ROM, complete the following activities:

1.  Study the flash cards for Chapter 15 to review the key terms in this chapter.

2.  Solve the hangman activities for Chapter 15.

3.  Complete the quiz in test mode for Chapter 15. Record your score in the space below, and print out your results for your instructor.

| |
|---|
| **StudyWARE Quiz Chapter 15** |
| Date Taken: _____ |
| Score: _____ |